LANGUAGE ARTS

WEEKLY

PRACTICE

Kindergarten

Credits
Author: Abby Farris
Copy Editor: Elise Craver

Visit *carsondellosa.com* for correlations to Common Core, state, national, and Canadian provincial standards.

Carson-Dellosa Publishing, LLC
PO Box 35665
Greensboro, NC 27425 USA
carsondellosa.com

978-1-4838-2788-9
01-053167784

Table of Contents

Introduction. 3

About This Book. 3

Common Core State Standards Alignment Matrix 4

School to Home Communication 6

Daily Extension Activities. 7

Week 1 17

Week 2. 21

Week 3. 25

Week 4. 29

Week 5. 33

Week 6. 37

Week 7. 41

Week 8. 45

Week 9. 49

Week 10. 53

Week 11. 57

Week 12. 61

Week 13. 65

Week 14. 69

Week 15. 73

Week 16. 77

Week 17. 81

Week 18. 85

Week 19. 89

Week 20. 93

Week 21. 97

Week 22. 101

Week 23. 105

Week 24. 109

Week 25. 113

Week 26. 117

Week 27. 121

Week 28. 125

Week 29. 129

Week 30. 133

Week 31. 137

Week 32. 141

Week 33. 145

Week 34. 149

Week 35. 153

Week 36. 157

Week 37. 161

Week 38. 165

Week 39. 169

Week 40. 173

Flash Cards. 177

Answer Key. 181

Introduction

The Weekly Practice series provides 40 weeks of essential daily practice in either math or language arts. It is the perfect supplement to any classroom curriculum and provides standards-based activities for every day of the week but Friday.

The activities are intended as homework assignments for Monday through Thursday and cover a wide spectrum of standards-based skills. The skills are presented at random to provide comprehensive learning but are repeated systematically throughout the book. The intention is to offer regular, focused practice to ensure mastery and retention.

Each 192-page book provides 40 weeks of reproducible pages, a standards alignment matrix, flash cards, and an answer key. The reproducible pages are perfect for homework but also work well for morning work, early finishers, and warm-up activities.

About This Book

Each page contains a variety of short, fun exercises that build in difficulty across the span of the book. The activities are divided into two sections:

• The Daily Extension Activities at the front of the book are intended to engage both student and family. These off-the-page activities are simple and fun so that students will look forward to this practice time at home. The activities span one week at a time. The instructions are clear and simple so that students can follow them with or without assistance in their homes. None need be returned to school.

• The daily practice section involves more comprehensive learning. Because of the simplicity of directions and straightforward tasks, students will be able to complete most tasks independently in a short period of time. There are four pages of activities per week, allowing for testing or a student break on Friday if desired. These pages are intended to be brought back to school.

Pages can be offered in any order, making it possible to reinforce specific skills when needed. However, skills are repeated regularly throughout the book to ensure retention over time, making a strong case for using pages sequentially.

An answer key is included for the daily practice section. You can check answers as a group for a quick follow-up lesson or monitor students' progress individually. Follow the basic page layout provided at the beginning of the answer key to match answers to page placement. Also included in the book is a set of flash cards. Reproduce them to give to students for at-home practice, or place them in classroom centers.

Common Core State Standards
Alignment Matrix

Standard	W1	W2	W3	W4	W5	W6	W7	W8	W9	W10	W11	W12	W13	W14	W15	W16	W17	W18	W19	W20
K.RL.1		●	●	●	●	●	●	●	●	●	●									
K.RL.2																				
K.RL.3												●	●	●	●	●	●	●	●	●
K.RL.4																				
K.RL.5																				
K.RL.6																				
K.RL.7																				
K.RL.9																				
K.RL.10																				
K.RI.1																				
K.RI.2																				
K.RI.3																				
K.RI.4																				
K.RI.5																				
K.RI.6																				
K.RI.7																				
K.RI.8																				
K.RI.9																				
K.RI.10																				
K.RF.1	●	●	●	●	●	●	●	●	●	●	●	●	●	●	●	●	●	●	●	●
K.RF.2	●	●	●	●	●	●	●	●	●	●	●	●	●	●	●	●	●	●	●	●
K.RF.3	●	●	●	●	●	●	●	●	●	●	●	●	●	●	●	●	●	●	●	●
K.RF.4																				
K.W.1		●	●	●	●	●	●	●	●	●	●	●	●	●	●	●	●	●	●	●
K.W.2	●	●	●	●	●	●	●	●	●	●	●	●	●	●	●	●	●	●	●	●
K.W.3																					●
K.W.4																				
K.W.5																				
K.W.6																				
K.W.7																				
K.W.8																				
K.L.1	●	●	●	●	●	●	●	●	●	●	●	●	●	●	●	●	●	●	●	●
K.L.2	●	●	●	●	●	●	●	●	●	●	●	●	●	●	●	●	●	●	●	●
K.L.4																				
K.L.5	●	●	●	●	●	●	●	●	●	●	●	●	●	●	●	●	●	●	●	●
K.L.6																				

W = Week

Common Core State Standards
Alignment Matrix

Standard	W21	W22	W23	W24	W25	W26	W27	W28	W29	W30	W31	W32	W33	W34	W35	W36	W37	W38	W39	W40
K.RL.1																				
K.RL.2												•	•	•	•	•	•	•	•	•
K.RL.3	•	•	•	•	•	•	•	•	•	•	•									
K.RL.4																				
K.RL.5																				
K.RL.6																				
K.RL.7																				
K.RL.9											•	•	•	•	•	•	•	•	•	•
K.RL.10																				
K.RI.1																				
K.RI.2																				
K.RI.3																				
K.RI.4																				
K.RI.5																				
K.RI.6																				
K.RI.7																				
K.RI.8																				
K.RI.9																				
K.RI.10																				
K.RF.1	•	•	•	•	•	•														
K.RF.2	•	•	•	•	•	•	•	•	•	•	•	•	•	•	•	•	•	•	•	•
K.RF.3	•	•	•	•	•	•	•	•	•	•	•	•	•	•	•	•	•	•	•	•
K.RF.4																				
K.W.1	•	•	•	•	•	•	•	•	•	•	•	•	•	•	•	•	•	•	•	•
K.W.2		•	•	•	•	•	•	•	•	•	•	•	•	•	•	•	•	•	•	•
K.W.3	•	•	•	•	•	•	•	•	•	•	•	•	•	•	•	•	•	•	•	•
K.W.5																				
K.W.6																				
K.W.7																				
K.W.8																				
K.L.1	•	•	•	•	•	•	•	•	•	•	•	•	•	•	•	•	•	•	•	•
K.L.2	•	•	•	•	•	•	•	•	•	•	•	•	•	•	•	•	•	•	•	•
K.L.4															•	•	•	•	•	•
K.L.5	•	•	•	•	•	•	•	•	•	•	•	•	•	•	•	•	•	•	•	•
K.L.6																				

W = Week

School to Home Communication

The research is clear that family involvement is strongly linked to student success. Support for student learning at home improves student achievement in school. Educators should not underestimate the significance of this connection.

The activities in this book create an opportunity to create or improve this school-to-home link. The activities span a week at a time and can be sent home as a week-long homework packet each Monday. Simply clip together the strip of fun activities from the front of the book with the pages for Days 1 to 4 for the correct week.

Most of the activities can be completed independently, but many encourage feedback or interaction with a family member. The activities are simple and fun, aiming to create a brief pocket of learning that is enjoyable to all.

In order to make the school-to-home program work for students and their families, we encourage you to reach out to them with an introductory letter. Explain the program and its intent and ask them to partner with you in their children's educational process. Describe the role you expect them to play. Encourage them to offer suggestions or feedback along the way.

A sample letter is included below. Use it as is or create your own letter to introduce this project and elicit their collaboration.

Dear Families,

I anticipate a productive and exciting year of learning and look forward to working with you and your child. We have a lot of work to do! I hope we—teacher, student, and family—can work together as a team to achieve the goal of academic progress we all hope for this year.

I will send home a packet of homework each week on _____. There will be two items to complete each day: a single task on a strip plus a full page of focused practice. Each page or strip is labeled Day 1 (for Monday), Day 2, Day 3, or Day 4. There is no homework on Friday.

Please make sure that your student brings back the completed work _____. It is important that these are brought in on time as we may work on some of the lessons as a class.

If you have any questions about this program or would like to talk to me about it, please feel free to call or email me. Thank you for joining me in making this the best year ever for your student!

Sincerely,

_____
Name

_____
Phone

_____
Email

	Day 1	Day 2	Day 3	Day 4
Week 1	Rainbow write your name with crayons five times on a sheet of paper. Then, spell your name aloud without looking at it.	Search at home for things that begin with the same letter as your name. How many objects did you find that begin with the same letter as your name?	Have an adult help you read the words. Tell which word does not rhyme with the other words. **bat fat mat sat pan rat**	Write each letter of your name on an index card. Put the cards in a bag. Shake the bag. Pull out one card at a time and tell the sound(s) that the letter makes.

	Day 1	Day 2	Day 3	Day 4
Week 2	Use play dough to form the letters in your name. Then, tell the sound that each letter in your name makes.	Search at home for things that are red. How many different objects did you find that are red?	Have an adult help you read the words. Tell which word does not rhyme with the other words. **let get met sit pet wet**	Write each lowercase and uppercase letter of the alphabet on separate index cards. Mix them up. Then, match them to make pairs.

	Day 1	Day 2	Day 3	Day 4
Week 3	Use yarn or string to form the letters in your name. Then, form the letters in the names of your family members.	Search at home for things that are blue. How many different objects did you find that are blue?	Have an adult help you read the words. Tell which word does not rhyme with the other words. **kit fit lid hit pit bit**	Write each letter of the alphabet on an index card. Put the cards in a bag. Shake the bag. Pull out one card at a time and tell the sound(s) that the letter makes.

	Day 1	Day 2	Day 3	Day 4
Week 4	Use chalk to write the letters in your name on a driveway or sidewalk. Then, tell the sound that each letter in your name makes.	Search at home for things that are yellow. How many different objects did you find that are yellow?	Have an adult help you read the words. Tell which word does not rhyme with the other words. **bun fun nut sun pun run**	Draw and name things around your home that are red and blue. Try to write a beginning sound for each picture.

	Day 1	Day 2	Day 3	Day 4
Week 5	Read the number word below. Hop on one foot that number of times. Then, say a word that rhymes with it. **two**	Search at home for things that are green. How many different objects did you find that are green?	Have an adult help you read the rhyming words. Then, say one more word that also rhymes with them. **cot tot got hot pot lot**	Name and draw things around your home that are yellow and green. Try to write a beginning sound for each picture.

	Day 1	Day 2	Day 3	Day 4
Week 6	Read the number word below. Clap your hands that number of times. Then, say a word that rhymes with it. **three**	Search at home for things that are orange. How many different objects did you find that are orange?	Have an adult help you read the rhyming words. Then, say one more word that also rhymes with them. **van tan man fan pan ran**	Write the color word **orange** on an index card. See, say, and spell the word aloud without looking at it.

	Day 1	Day 2	Day 3	Day 4
Week 7	Read the number word below. Tap your knees that number of times. Then, say a word that rhymes with it. **one**	Search at home for things that are purple. How many different objects did you find that are purple?	Have an adult help you read the rhyming words. Then, say one more word that also rhymes with them. **rig dig wig fig pig jig**	Write the color word **purple** on an index card. See, say, and spell the word aloud without looking at it.

	Day 1	Day 2	Day 3	Day 4
Week 8	Read the number word below. Nod your head that number of times. Then, say a word that rhymes with it. **five**	Search at home for things that are brown. How many different objects did you find that are brown?	Have an adult help you read the rhyming words. Then, say one more word that also rhymes with them. **led bed wed fed Ned Ted**	Write the color word **brown** on an index card. See, say, and spell the word aloud without looking at it.

	Day 1	Day 2	Day 3	Day 4
Week 9	Read the number word below. Blink your eyes that number of times. Then, tell a word that rhymes with it. **six**	Search at home for things that are black. How many different objects did you find that are black?	Identify the letters and say the sound of each. Try to name objects in your kitchen that begin with each of the letters. **m b c s f e**	Write the color word **black** on an index card. See, say, and spell the word aloud without looking at it.
Week 10	Read the number word below. Stomp your feet that number of times. Then, tell a word that rhymes with it. **four**	Search at home for things that are pink. How many different objects did you find that are pink?	Identify the letters and say the sound of each one. Try to name objects in your family room that begin with each of the letters. **p v c a d l**	Write the color word **pink** on an index card. See, say, and spell the word aloud without looking at it.
Week 11	Read the number word below. Shrug your shoulders that number of times. Then, tell a word that rhymes with it. **nine**	Search at home for things that are white. How many different objects did you find that are white?	Identify the letters and say the sound of each one. Try to name objects in your bedroom that begin with each of the letters. **b r c y t d**	Write the color word **white** on an index card. See, say, and spell the word aloud without looking at it.
Week 12	Read the number word below. Swing your arms that number of times. Then, tell a word that rhymes with it. **seven**	Search outside your home for objects that begin with each letter of the alphabet. See how many things you can find in five minutes.	Identify the letters and say the sound of each one. Try to name objects in your bathroom that begin with each of the letters. **k l m p s t**	Name and draw things around your home that are orange, purple, and brown. Try to write a beginning sound for each picture.

	Day 1	Day 2	Day 3	Day 4
Week 13	Read the number word. Hop on both feet that number of times. Then, say a word that rhymes with it. **ten**	Search outside for objects that begin with each letter of the alphabet. See how many things you can find in five minutes.	Read the rhyme. Change the bold words to other rhyming words. Little bitty **bee**, Can you see **me**? Look in the **tree**. What could I **be**?	Name and draw things around your home that are black, pink, and white. Try to write a beginning sound for each picture.
	Day 1	Day 2	Day 3	Day 4
Week 14	Read the number word. Touch your toes that number of times. Then, say a word that rhymes with it. **eight**	Search at the grocery store for objects that begin with each letter of the alphabet. See how many things you can find in five minutes.	Read the rhyme. Change the bold words to other rhyming words. The frog will **snap**, He forgot his **cap**. Here is his **map**, Now, he will **nap**.	Read the sight words. Rainbow write them with different colored crayons. Then, spell each word aloud without looking. **how can at the**
	Day 1	Day 2	Day 3	Day 4
Week 15	Read the number word. Wiggle your nose that number of times. Then, say a word that rhymes with it. **zero**	Look through a picture book. Search for objects that end with the letters **m**, **p**, **d**, and **b**. See how many things you can find.	Read the rhyme. Change the bold words to other rhyming words. The silly little **fly** Asked the nice **guy**, "Will you eat the **pie**, With a french **fry**?"	Read the sight words. Use a paintbrush to form the letters. Then, spell each word aloud without looking. **is some you be**
	Day 1	Day 2	Day 3	Day 4
Week 16	Clap each syllable in the words **rag**, **beg**, **wig**, **fog**, and **jug**. Then, name as many words as you can that have one syllable.	Look through a picture book at home. Search for objects that end with the letters **t**, **n**, **r**, and **g**. See how many things you can find.	Practice separating sounds by tapping out the letter sounds in each word. Then, blend the sounds. Say each word. **cat get hit pot nut**	Use yarn or string to form the letters in the sight words. Then, spell each word aloud without looking. **are that I see**

	Day 1	Day 2	Day 3	Day 4
Week 17	Clap each syllable in the words **ladder**, **pepper**, **himself**, **sunshine**, and **meatball**. Then, name more words that have two syllables.	Look through a picture book. Search for objects that end with the letters **s**, **c**, **k**, **l**, and **x**. See how many things you can find.	Practice separating sounds by tapping out the letter sounds in each word. Then, blend the sounds. Say each word. **lap pep dip top pup**	Read the sight words. Form each letter on a friend's back to spell the words. Then, spell each word aloud without looking. **we said and do**
Week 18	Clap each syllable in the words **ladybug**, **telephone**, **dinosaur**, **potato**, and **umbrella**. Then, name more words that have three syllables.	Tell a family member about a book that you listened to or read on your own at school today. Tell them about your favorite part and why.	Practice separating sounds by tapping out the letter sounds in each word. Then, blend the sounds. Say each word. **van ten pin con run**	Fill a plate with flour. Draw the letters in the flour to spell the words. Then, spell each word aloud without looking. **will my what it**
Week 19	Clap each syllable in the words **alligator**, **helicopter**, **caterpillar**, **watermelon**, and **macaroni**. Then, name more words that have four syllables.	Tell a family member about a book that you listened to or read on your own at school today. Tell them about a new word you learned.	Practice separating sounds by tapping out the letter sounds in each word. Then, blend the sounds. Say each word. **lad bed hid nod dud**	Read the sight words. Form each letter in the air to spell the sight words. Then, spell each word aloud without looking. **like than did her**
Week 20	Draw a picture of your weekend. Write one to three sentences to go along with your picture. Focus on putting spaces between your words.	Tell a family member about a book that you listened to or read on your own. Tell them about a part you did not understand. Ask them to explain it to you.	Practice separating sounds by tapping out the letter sounds in each word. Then, blend the sounds. Say each word. **rag beg wig fog jug**	Read the sight words. Use ABC blocks or letter tiles to spell the words. Then, spell each word aloud without looking. **have but for in**

	Day 1	Day 2	Day 3	Day 4
Week 21	Draw a picture of your favorite book. Write one to three sentences to go along with your picture. Focus on putting spaces between your words.	Tell an adult about a book that you listened to or read on your own at school today. Describe one of the characters with two adjectives.	Read the words. Tell a family member which words have a short vowel sound. **mop pine fin tote cap bite**	Use sidewalk chalk to rainbow write the sight words. Then, spell each word aloud without looking. **little up all me**
Week 22	Draw a picture of your favorite snack. Write one to three sentences to go along with your picture. Focus on putting spaces between your words.	Tell an adult about a book that you listened to or read on your own at school today. Tell them what the character may have learned.	Read the words. Tell a family member which words have a short vowel sound. **note rip cane hop kit rate**	Use yarn to form the letters and spell the sight words. Then, spell each word aloud without looking. **where she on his**
Week 23	Draw a picture of a TV show. Write one to three sentences to go along with your picture. Focus on using capital letters at the beginning of each sentence.	Tell an adult about a book that you listened to or read on your own at school today. Describe two characters with two adjectives each.	Read the words. Tell a family member which words have a short vowel sound. **tap mute con cope cut rat**	Use cotton swabs and paint to dot out each letter and spell the words. Then, spell each word aloud without looking. **make no was or**
Week 24	Draw a picture of a favorite toy. Write one to three sentences to go along with your picture. Focus on using capital letters at the beginning of each sentence.	Tell an adult about a book that you listened to or read on your own at school today. Retell the story from beginning to end.	Read the words. Tell a family member which words have a long vowel sound. **mope pin bit cute fine not**	Use magnetic letters on a cookie tray to spell the words. Then, spell each word aloud without looking. **when not them if**

	Day 1	Day 2	Day 3	Day 4
Week 25	Draw a picture of a special game. Write one to three sentences to go along with your picture. Focus on using capital letters at the beginning of each sentence.	Tell an adult about a book that you listened to or read on your own at school today. Tell them about what you learned about one of the characters.	Read the words. Tell a family member which words have a long vowel sound. **hope mutt tape kite cop ripe**	Cut out letters in a magazine to spell each sight word. Then, spell each word aloud without looking. **they has with so**
Week 26	Draw a picture of your favorite place. Write one to three sentences to go along with your picture. Focus on putting a period at the end of each sentence.	Tell an adult about a book that you listened to or read on your own at school today. Try to act out the story from the beginning to the end.	Read the words. Tell a family member which words have a long vowel sound. **cone can cape lip bribe tot**	Use toothpicks to form the letters and spell the sight words. Then, spell each word aloud without looking. **been him this he**
Week 27	Draw a picture of your favorite dessert. Write three sentences to go along with your picture. Focus on putting a period at the end of each sentence.	Choose a fiction book from home to read with an adult. Discuss the parts of a fiction book.	With an adult, search in your kitchen for objects that have short vowel sounds in the middle. See how many things you can find in five minutes.	Use cooked spaghetti noodles to form the letters and spell the sight words. Then, spell each word aloud without looking. **who had other a**
Week 28	Draw a picture of a special friend. Write three sentences to go along with your picture. Focus on putting a period at the end of each sentence.	Choose a nonfiction book from home to read with an adult. Discuss the parts of a nonfiction book.	Search in your bedroom for objects that have short vowel sounds in the middle. See how many things you can find in five minutes.	Use play dough to form the letters and spell the sight words. Then, spell each word aloud without looking. **about then of as**

	Day 1	Day 2	Day 3	Day 4
Week 29	Draw a picture of your favorite movie. Write three sentences to go along with your picture. Focus on using descriptive words in each sentence.	Choose a fiction book from home to read with an adult. Discuss what the author and illustrator do.	Search in your family room for objects that have short vowel sounds in the middle. See how many things you can find in five minutes.	Use yarn or string to form the letters to spell the sight words. Then, spell each word aloud without looking. **were into** **one am**

	Day 1	Day 2	Day 3	Day 4
Week 30	Draw a picture of a spring day. Write three sentences to go along with your picture. Focus on using descriptive words in each sentence.	Choose a nonfiction book from home to read with an adult. Discuss what the author and illustrator do.	Search in your bathroom for objects that have long vowel sounds in the middle. See how many things you can find in five minutes.	Use glue to form the letters to spell the sight words. Sprinkle glitter on the words. Then, spell each word aloud without looking. **which out** **to your**

	Day 1	Day 2	Day 3	Day 4
Week 31	Draw a picture of how you can take care of Earth. Write three or more informational sentences to go along with your picture.	Choose a fiction book from home to read with an adult. Discuss key details from the book.	Search the refrigerator for objects that have long vowel sounds in the middle. See how many things you can find in five minutes.	Cheer or rap each letter to spell the sight words. Then, spell each word aloud without looking. **there each** **by an**

	Day 1	Day 2	Day 3	Day 4
Week 32	Draw a picture of an animal found in a pond. Write three sentences to go along with your picture. Focus on using descriptive words in each sentence.	Choose a nonfiction book from home to read with an adult. Discuss key details from the book.	Search in your toy box for objects that have long vowel sounds in the middle. See how many things you can find in five minutes.	Use a marker to dot out each letter to spell the sight words. Then, spell each word aloud without looking. **why these** **more**

	Day 1	**Day 2**	**Day 3**	**Day 4**
Week 33	Draw a picture of what the weather is like today. Write three or more informational sentences to go along with your picture.	Choose a fiction book from home to read with an adult. Compare and contrast it to a previously read book.	Add a silent **e** to the end of each word to make a new word. Read each new word. **pin + e =** **hop + e =** **rat + e =** **fin + e =**	Use alphabet magnets to spell the sight words. Then, spell each word aloud without looking. **many would from**
Week 34	Draw a picture of a zoo animal. Write or tell a fictional short story to go along with your picture.	Choose a nonfiction book from home to read with an adult. Compare and contrast it to a previously read book.	Add a silent **e** to the end of each word to make a new word. Read each new word. **tap + e =** **con + e =** **rip + e =** **not + e =**	Write each letter of the alphabet on separate index cards. Put them in a bag. Shake the bag and pull out 10 cards. See how many words you can make.
Week 35	Draw a picture of an ocean animal. Write three or more informational sentences to go along with your picture.	Choose a fiction book from home to read with an adult. Connect it to a real-life story.	Add the letter **s** to the end of each word to make a new word. Read each new word. **mop + s =** **can + s =** **jar + s =** **kit + s =**	Write each letter of the alphabet on separate index cards. Put them in a bag. Shake the bag and pull out 10 cards. See how many words you can make.
Week 36	Draw a picture of an insect. Write or tell a fictional short story to go along with your picture.	Choose an informational book from home to read with an adult. Connect it to a real-life story.	Add the letter **s** to the end of each word to make a new word. Read each new word. **bag + s =** **pen + s =** **letter + s =** **toy + s =**	Write each letter of the alphabet on separate index cards. Put them in a bag. Shake the bag and pull out 10 cards. See how many words you can make.

	Day 1	**Day 2**	**Day 3**	**Day 4**
Week 37	Draw a picture of a family member. Write three or more informational sentences to go along with your picture.	Choose a fiction book to read with an adult. Tell how you know it is fiction.	Replace the first sound in **hop** with the the /t/ sound to make a new word. Replace the first sound in **tan** with the the /f/ sound to make a new word.	Separate the sounds of the words by tapping out each sound. Remember that digraphs make one sound. **thumb chin ship sock whisk**
Week 38	Draw a picture of outer space. Write or tell a fictional short story to go along with your picture.	Choose a nonfiction book to read with an adult. Tell how you know it is an informational book.	Replace the first sound in **hop** with the /m/ sound to make a new word. Replace the first sound in **sit** with the /k/ sound to make a new word.	Separate the sounds of the words by tapping out each sound. Remember that digraphs make one sound. **think chap shot pack whale**
Week 39	Draw a picture of your favorite memory from kindergarten. Write three or more informational sentences to go along with your picture.	Choose a fiction book to read with an adult. Write a different ending for it.	Replace the last sound in **ham** with the /t/ sound to make a new word. Replace the last sound in **tap** with the /g/ sound to make a new word.	Separate the sounds of the words by tapping out each sound. Remember that digraphs make one sound. **their cheer shell sick where**
Week 40	Draw a picture about what you learned in kindergarten today. Write three or more informational sentences to go along with your picture.	Choose a nonfiction book to read with an adult. Write a new title for it.	Replace the last sound in **kit** with the /d/ sound to make a new word. Replace the last sound in **rod** with the /t/ sound to make a new word.	Separate the sounds of the words by tapping out each sound. Remember that digraphs make one sound. **thirst luck share chain whistle**

Write your name. Start with a capital letter. Hold your pencil properly.

_____

– – – – – – – – – – – – – – – –

_____

Draw a picture of a school tool that you used today.

Circle the letters in your name.

a	b	c	d	e	f	g
h	i	j	k	l	m	n
o	p	q	r	s	t	u
v	w	x	y	z		

Sort the letters.

A   b   c   D   E   f

Lowercase	Uppercase

Circle the pictures whose names rhyme.

Draw an **X** on the picture that does not belong.

Draw a face to show how you felt on the first day of school.

Sort the letters and numbers.

a   2   G   k   6   4

Letters	Numbers

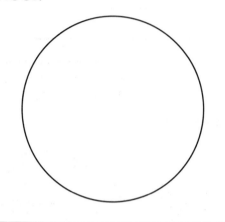

_____
- - - -
____pple

Draw a square around the pictures whose names rhyme with **van**.

    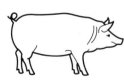

Practice writing your name with your favorite color crayon.

- -

Circle the objects that are found in a classroom.

Draw an object that begins with the /a/ sound.

Draw an **X** on the words that do not rhyme with **cat**.

bat

mug

mat

sat

pan

Sort the letters and numbers.

3   N   7   5   s   W

Letters	Numbers

Trace and write the letters **Aa**.

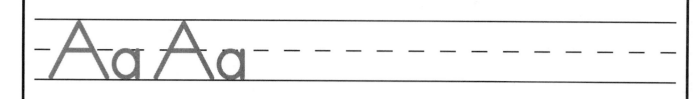

Sort the letters and numbers.

j   q   L   8   4   c

Letters	Numbers

Draw an object that rhymes with **cat**.

Draw an **X** on the words that do not rhyme with **pan**.

van

lip

ran

tan

sap

Circle the pictures that show things you do at school.

Write your first and last names. Start with a capital letter. Use a red crayon.

_____

— — — — — — — — — —

_____

— — — — — — — — — —

_____

Draw a picture of something you see in summer.

Draw lines to match the letters.

a   E

C   g

e   c

G   A

Sort the letters.

G   h   I   j   K   l   M

Lowercase	Uppercase

Circle the pictures whose names rhyme.

Draw an **X** on the picture that does not belong.

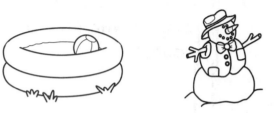

Draw a picture of an object that is red. Color it red.

Read a book with an adult. Write the title.

_____

— — — — — — — — — — —

_____

_____

— — — — — — — — — — —

_____

_____

— — —

_____at

Draw a square around the pictures whose names rhyme with **I**.

Practice writing the color word **red**.

Use a red crayon to circle the objects that are red.

Draw an object that begins with the /b/ sound.

Draw an **X** on the words that do not rhyme with **pet**.

set	fog
bug	bet
sit	pet
let	hug

Read each word with an adult. Circle the words with one syllable in red. Circle the words with two syllables in blue.

belly	ball
cab	candy

Trace and write the letters **Bb**.

BbBb

Think about a book you listened to this week. Draw your favorite part.

Stomp the number of words in the sentence. Write the number.

The ball is red.

_____

Draw an **X** on the words that do not rhyme with **big**.

wig   bin

pig   fig

pop   sag

dig   log

Circle the pictures that show things you do outside.

Write a friend's name. Start with a capital letter. Use a blue crayon.

_____

– – – – – – – – – – – – – – – –

_____

Draw a picture of something you hear in summer.

Draw lines to match the letters.

b   F

D   B

f   h

H   d

Sort the letters.

n   O   p   Q   r   S

Lowercase	Uppercase

Circle the pictures whose names rhyme.

2

Draw an **X** on the picture that does not belong.

Draw a picture of an object that is blue. Color it blue.

Read a book with an adult. Write the title.

_____

- - - - - - - - - - - - - - - - - - -

_____

- - - - - - - - - - - - - - - - - - -

_____

_____

- - - -

_____at

Draw a square around the pictures whose names rhyme with **bake**.

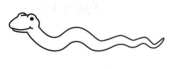

Practice writing the color word **blue**.

_____

— — — — — — — — — — — — — — — — — — —

_____

Use a blue crayon to circle the objects that are blue.

Draw an object that begins with **c**. It should start with the /k/ sound or the /s/ sound.

Draw an **X** on the words that do not rhyme with **fun**.

fox	**bun**
wig	**run**
pun	**jug**
sun	**dog**

Read each word with an adult. Circle the words with one syllable in red. Circle the words with two syllables in blue.

dog	**tiger**
basket	**mop**

Trace and write the letters **Cc**.

CcCc

Think about a book you listened to this week. Draw your favorite part.

Clap the number of words in the sentence. Write the number.

The car is blue.

_____

Draw an **X** on the words that do not rhyme with **bed**.

lad   fed

led   car

red   wed

bus   tub

Circle the pictures that show things you like to do.

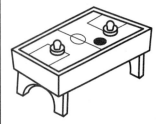
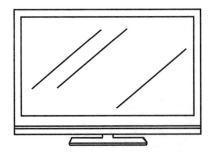

Write a pet's name. Start with a capital letter. Use a yellow crayon.

_____

_ _ _ _ _ _ _ _ _ _ _ _ _ _ _

_____

Draw a picture of something you taste in summer.

Draw lines to match the letters.

m   K

L   j

J   l

k   M

Sort the letters.

t   U   v   W   x   Y   z

Lowercase	Uppercase

Circle the pictures whose names rhyme.

Draw an **X** on the picture that does not belong.

Draw a picture of an object that is yellow. Color it yellow.

Read a book with an adult. Write the title.

_____

- - - - - - - - - - - - - - - - -

_____

- - - - - - - - - - - - - - - - -

_____

____
- - -
_____og

Draw a square around the pictures whose names rhyme with **nice**.

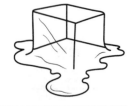

Practice writing the color word **yellow**.

_____

– – – – – – – – – – – – – – – –

_____

Use a yellow crayon to circle the objects that are yellow.

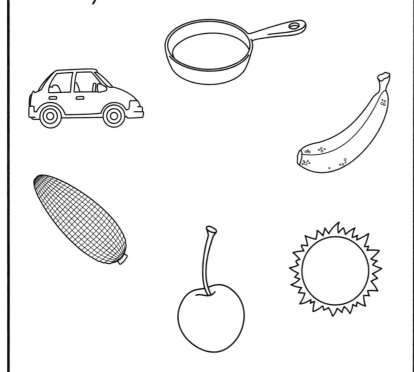

Draw an object that begins with the /d/ sound.

Draw an **X** on the words that do not rhyme with **ship**.

dip	**shoe**
get	**hip**
lip	**bob**
sip	**tip**

Read each word with an adult. Circle the words with one syllable in yellow. Circle the words with two syllables in green.

robot	**frog**
ball	**baby**

Trace and write the letters **Dd**.

Think about a book you listened to this week. Draw your favorite part.

Tap the number of words in the sentence. Write the number.

The bird is yellow.

_____

Draw an **X** on the words that do not rhyme with **rug**.

chair	bug
dug	bee
hug	cot
mug	mouse

Circle the pictures that show things you plan to do this weekend.

Write a family member's name. Start with a capital letter. Use a green crayon.

_____

– – – – – – – – – – – – –

_____

Draw a picture of something you smell in summer.

Draw lines to match the letters.

i   P

N   I

p   n

R   r

Write the word for each picture. The words should rhyme.

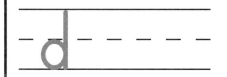

Draw a line to connect each picture to the letter of its beginning sound.

   s

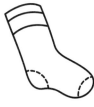   d

2   b

          t

Name _____

Draw an **X** on the picture that does not belong.

Draw a picture of an object that is green. Color it green.

Read a book with an adult. Write the title.

_____
‑ ‑ ‑ ‑ ‑ ‑ ‑ ‑ ‑ ‑ ‑ ‑ ‑ ‑
_____

_____
‑ ‑ ‑ ‑ ‑ ‑ ‑ ‑ ‑ ‑ ‑ ‑ ‑ ‑
_____

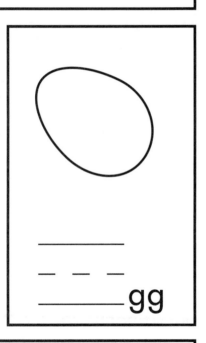

_____
‑ ‑ ‑
_____gg

Write a sentence telling why broccoli is not a dessert.

_____
‑ ‑ ‑ ‑ ‑ ‑ ‑ ‑ ‑ ‑ ‑ ‑ ‑ ‑
_____

_____
‑ ‑ ‑ ‑ ‑ ‑ ‑ ‑ ‑ ‑ ‑ ‑ ‑ ‑
_____

Practice writing the color word **green**.

_____

– – – – – – – – – – – – – – – – – – –

_____

Use a green crayon to circle the objects that are green.

Draw an object that begins with the /e/ sound.

Circle each **A** and **a**.

Q	w	A	e
a	R	u	T
a	F	v	A
s	d	x	a

Read each word with an adult. Circle the words with one syllable in yellow. Circle the words with two syllables in green.

boat   **driveway**

garage   **dish**

Trace and write the letters **Ee**.

Think about a book you listened to this week. Draw your favorite part.

Snap the number of words in the sentence. Write the number.

A green frog hopped.

_____

Draw two objects whose names rhyme.

Circle the pictures that show things you like to do in school.

Write your teacher's name. Start with a capital letter. Use an orange crayon.

_____

– – – – – – – – – – – – – – – – – –

_____

– – – – – – – – – – – – – – – – – –

_____

Draw a picture of something you do in summer.

Draw lines to match the letters.

o   q

Q   S

s   u

U   O

Draw a line to connect each picture to the letter of its beginning sound.

b

c

m

f

Write the word for each picture. The words should rhyme.

m _____

t _____

37

Draw an **X** on the picture that does not belong.

Draw a picture of an object that is orange. Color it orange.

Read a book with an adult. Write the author's name.

_____

- - - - - - - - - - - - - -

_____

_____

- - - - - - - - - - - - - -

_____

_____

- - - -

_____ish

Write a sentence telling about a costume you like to wear.

_____

- -

_____

_____

- -

_____

Practice writing the color word **orange**.

_____

— — — — — — — — — — — — — — — — — —

_____

Use an orange crayon to circle the objects that are orange.

Draw an object that begins with the /f/ sound.

Circle each **B** and **b**.

b	F	v	B
s	d	x	a
g	h	J	b
z	L	c	B

Read each word with an adult. Circle the words with one syllable in orange. Circle the words with two syllables in purple.

window   **door**

chair   **table**

Trace and write the letters **Ff**.

F f   F f   — — — — — — — — —

Think about a book you listened to this week.
Draw your favorite part.

Stomp the number of words in the sentence. Write the number.

The orange dripped on me.

_____

Draw two objects whose names rhyme.

Write the sentence correctly.

the ball is rid

Write the name of a neighbor. Start with a capital letter. Use a purple crayon.

_____

— — — — — — — — — — — —

_____

— — — — — — — — — — — —

_____

Draw a picture of something you see in autumn.

Draw lines to match the letters.

t   Z

V   X

x   v

z   T

Draw a line to connect each picture to the letter of its beginning sound.

f

v

h

s

Write the word for each picture. The words should rhyme.

h _____

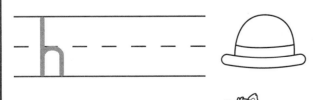

c _____

Draw an **X** on the pictures that do not belong.

Draw a picture of an object that is purple. Color it purple.

Read a book with an adult. Write the title.

_____

_ _ _ _ _ _ _ _ _ _ _ _ _ _

_____

_ _ _ _ _ _ _ _ _ _ _ _ _ _

_____

_____

_ _ _ _

_____ame

Write a sentence telling which sport is your favorite.

_____

_ _ _ _ _ _ _ _ _ _ _ _ _ _

_____

_ _ _ _ _ _ _ _ _ _ _ _ _ _

_____

Practice writing the color word **purple**.

_____

_ _

_____

Use a purple crayon to circle the objects that are purple.

Draw an object that begins with the /g/ sound.

Circle each **C** and **c**.

a	F	v	C
s	d	x	c
v	c	N	m
k	C	i	z

Read each word with an adult. Circle the words with one syllable in orange. Circle the words with two syllables in purple.

happy   **rain**

sunshine   **sad**

Trace and write the letters **Gg**.

Gg Gg

Think about a book you listened to this week. Draw your favorite part.

Clap the number of words in the sentence. Write the number.

A purple sock is missing.

_____

Draw two objects whose names rhyme.

Write the sentence correctly.

the bleu car is fast

Write the name of your town. Start with a capital letter. Use a brown crayon.

_____

— — — — — — — —

_____

— — — — — — — —

_____

Draw a picture of something you hear in autumn.

Draw lines to match the letters.

w   W

b   y

Y   D

d   B

Draw a line to connect each picture to the letter of its beginning sound.

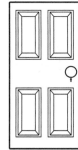

n

d

c

p

Write the word for each picture. The words should rhyme.

_____

v

_____

f

Draw an **X** on the pictures that do not belong.

Draw a picture of an object that is brown. Color it brown.

Read a book with an adult. Write the title.

_____

_ _ _

_____at

Write a sentence about the perfect fruit salad.

Practice writing the color word **brown**.

_____

— — — — — — — — — — — — — — — — — — — —

_____

Use a brown crayon to circle the objects that are brown.

Draw an object that begins with the /h/ sound.

Circle each **D** and **d**.

D	y	u	d
i	d	O	p
d	F	v	D
s	d	x	Y

Read each word with an adult. Circle the words with two syllables in brown. Circle the words with three syllables in black.

surprise   **potato**

hospital   **asleep**

Trace and write the letters **Hh**.

Hh Hh – – – – – – – – – – – – –

Think about a book you listened to this week. Draw your favorite part.

Tap the number of words in the sentence. Write the number.

My hair is brown.

_____

Draw two objects whose names rhyme.

Write the sentence correctly.

the bird is yelow

_____

Write your nickname. Start with a capital letter. Use a black crayon.

_____

— — — — — — — —

_____

— — — — — — — —

_____

Draw a picture of something you taste in autumn.

Circle the picture whose name has one syllable.

Draw a line to connect each picture to the letter of its beginning sound.

b

c

m

f

Draw a face to show how you feel today.

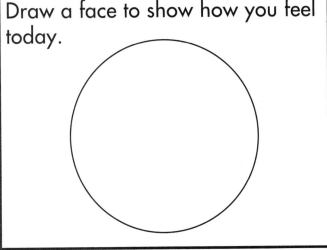

Draw an **X** on the pictures that do not belong.

Draw a picture of an object that is black. Color it black.

Read a book with an adult. Write the title.

_____

- - - - - - - - - - - - - - -

_____

_____

- - - - - - - - - - - - - - -

_____

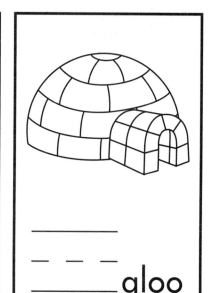

_____

- - - - gloo

Write a sentence telling something you would like to learn.

_____

- - - - - - - - - - - - - - -

_____

_____

- - - - - - - - - - - - - - -

_____

Practice writing the color word **black**.

_____

– – – – – – – – – – – – – – –

_____

Use a black crayon to circle the objects that are black.

Draw an object that begins with the /i/ sound.

Circle each **E** and **e**.

E   y   u   e

i   O   p   e

e   F   v   E

s   d   x   a

Read each word with an adult. Circle the words with two syllables in brown. Circle the words with three syllables in black.

grandpa   **apricot**

address   **piano**

Trace and write the letters **Ii**.

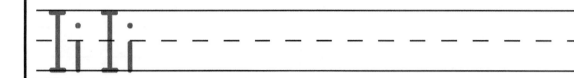

Think about a book you listened to this week. Draw your favorite part.

Snap the number of words in the sentence. Write the number.

My black dog has one white spot.

_____

Draw two objects whose names rhyme.

Write the sentence correctly.

a grene frog hopped on me

_____

– – – – – – – – – – – –

_____

_____

– – – – – – – – – – – –

_____

– – – – – – – – – – – –

_____

Write the name of a stuffed animal. Start with a capital letter. Use a pink crayon.

_____

– – – – – – – – – – – – – – – – – –

_____

– – – – – – – – – – – – – – – – – –

_____

Draw a picture of something you smell in autumn.

Circle the picture whose name has one syllable.

Draw a line to connect each picture to the letter of its beginning sound.

h

p

s

f

Draw a face to show how you feel at bedtime.

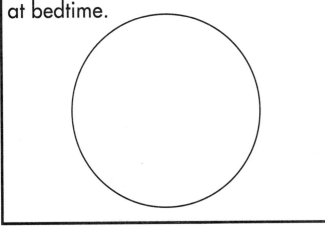

Draw an **X** on the pictures that do not belong.

Draw a picture of an object that is pink. Color it pink.

Read a book with an adult. Write the author's name.

_____

– – – – – – – – – – – – – – – –

_____

– – – – – – – – – – – – – – – –

_____

_____

– – – –

_____ug

Write a sentence about what you see in the sky at night.

_____

– – – – – – – – – – – – – – – –

_____

_____

– – – – – – – – – – – – – – – –

_____

Practice writing the color word **pink**.

_____

‒ ‒

_____

Use a pink crayon to circle the objects that are pink.

Draw an object that begins with the /j/ sound.

Circle each **F** and **f**.

F	y	u	f
i	O	p	K
v	B	N	m
k	F	i	f

Read each word with an adult. Circle the words with two syllables in red. Circle the words with three syllables in blue.

frozen   **fingernail**

spaghetti   **airplane**

Trace and write the letters **Jj**.

Think about a book you listened to this week. Draw your favorite part.

Stomp the number of words in the sentence. Write the number.

This shirt is bright pink.

_____

Draw two objects whose names rhyme.

Write the sentence correctly.

the oringe dripped on me

Write the name of your favorite restaurant. Start with a capital letter.

_____

— — — — — — — — — — — —

_____

— — — — — — — — — — — —

_____

Draw a picture of something you do in autumn.

Circle the picture whose name has one syllable.

Draw a face to show how you feel at the doctor.

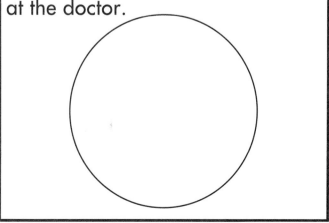

Draw a line to connect each picture to the letter of its beginning sound.

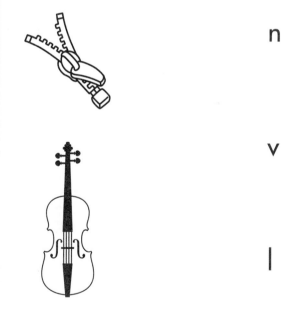

n

v

l

z

Draw an **X** on the pictures that do not belong.

Draw a picture of an object that is white. Outline it with a black crayon.

Read a book with an adult. Write the illustrator's name.

_____

_ _ _ _ _ _ _ _ _ _ _ _ _ _ _ _ _

_____

_ _ _ _ _ _ _ _ _ _ _ _ _ _ _ _ _

_____

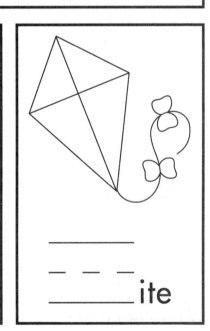

_____

_ _ _ _

_____ite

Write a sentence telling what is in a salad.

_____

_ _

_____

_____

_ _

_____

Practice writing the color word **white**.

_____

– – – – – – – – – – – – – – – –

_____

Circle the objects that are white.

Draw an object that begins with the /k/ sound.

Circle each **G** and **g**.

Q   w   G   e

g   r   T   G

y   u   g   i

k   G   i   g

Read each word with an adult. Circle the words with two syllables in yellow. Circle the words with three syllables in green.

library   **spelling**

officer   **apple**

Trace and write the letters **Kk**.

Kk Kk

Think about a book you listened to this week. Draw your favorite part.

Clap the number of words in the sentence. Write the number.

Yesterday was a very long day!

_____

Draw two objects whose names rhyme.

Write the sentence correctly.

a purple sock iz missing

Write your first and last name in your best handwriting.

_____

— — — — — — — — — — — —

_____

_____

— — — — — — — — — — — —

_____

Draw one thing you should do to stay safe in a fire.

Circle the pictures whose names have one syllable.

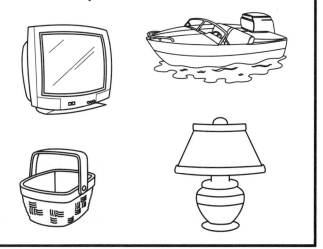

Draw a line to connect each picture to the letter of its beginning sound.

k

g

d

b

Draw a face to show how you feel in the dark.

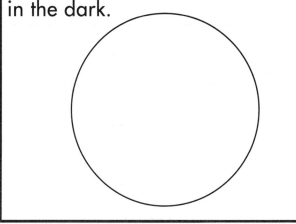

Circle the pictures that go together.

Read a fiction book with an adult. Draw a picture of one of the characters.

Read a fiction book with an adult. Write one character's name.

_____
_ _ _ _ _ _ _ _ _ _ _ _ _ _ _
_____
_ _ _ _ _ _ _ _ _ _ _ _ _ _ _
_____

_____
_ _ _ _
_____amp

Write a sentence about something that is the shape of a circle.

_____
_ _
_____
_ _
_____

What is the word without ✄? _____

_ _ _ _ _ _ _ _ _ _ _ _ _ _

_____

Complete the sentence.

One thing I should do to stay safe in a fire is

_____

_ _ _ _ _ _ _ _ _ _ _ _ _ _ _ _

_____

_____

_ _ _ _ _ _ _ _ _ _ _ _ _ _ _ _

_____

Draw an object that begins with the /l/ sound.

Read each word with an adult. Circle the words with two syllables in orange. Circle the words with three syllables in purple.

bicycle   **scissors**

strawberry   **skateboard**

Circle each **H** and **h**.

H   y   u   h

i   O   p   l

h   F   v   H

s   d   x   K

Trace and write the letters **Ll**.

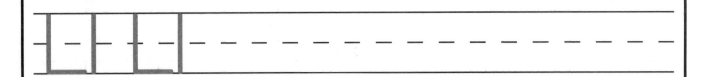

Think about a book you listened to this week. Draw your favorite part.

Write the missing letter in the color word. Color the crayon.

_____ed

Draw two objects whose names rhyme.

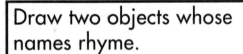

Write the sentence correctly.

is mi hair dark brown

Write the day of the week in your best handwriting.

_____

— — — — — — — — — — —

_____

Draw a picture of something you are thankful for.

Circle the picture whose name has two syllables.

Draw a line to connect each picture to the letter of its beginning sound.

w

h

p

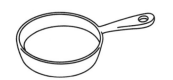

l

Draw a face to show how you feel when you play with a friend.

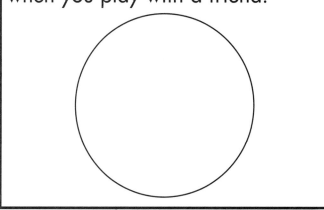

Circle the pictures that go together.

Read a fiction book with an adult. Draw a picture of one of the characters.

Read a fiction book with an adult. Write one character's name.

_____

_ _ _ _ _ _ _ _ _ _ _ _ _ _ _ _ _

_____

_ _ _ _ _ _ _ _ _ _ _ _ _ _ _ _ _

_____

_____

_ _ _ _

_____op

Write a sentence telling about what it might be like to live in a castle.

_____

_ _

_____

_ _

_____

What is the word without 🧈 ?

_____

_ _ _ _ _ _ _ _ _ _ _ _

_____

Complete the sentence.

I am thankful for

_____

_ _ _ _ _ _ _ _ _ _ _ _

_____

_____

_ _ _ _ _ _ _ _ _ _ _ _

_____

Draw an object that begins with the /m/ sound.

Read each word with an adult. Circle the words with two syllables in orange. Circle the words with three syllables in black.

pumpkin   **broccoli**

cucumber   **paper**

Circle each **I** and **i**.

I   y   u   a

J   i   O   p

X   F   v   I

s   d   i   a

Trace and write the letters **Mm**.

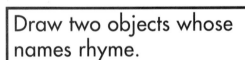

Think about a book you listened to this week.
Draw your favorite part.

Write the missing letter in the color word. Color the crayon.

bl __ e

Draw two objects whose names rhyme.

Write the sentence correctly.

i am going to be late

Write one classroom rule.

_____

— — — — — — — — — —

_____

— — — — — — — — — —

_____

Draw a picture of something you did this weekend.

Circle the picture whose name has two syllables.

Draw a line to connect each picture to the letter of its beginning sound.

y

r

h

t

Draw a face to show how you feel when you get hurt.

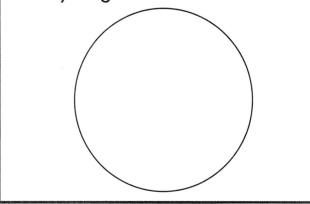

Circle the pictures that go together.

Read a fiction book with an adult. Draw a picture of one of the characters.

Read a fiction book with an adult. Write one character's name.

_____

_ _ _ _ _ _ _ _ _ _ _ _ _ _ _ _

_____

_ _ _ _ _ _ _ _ _ _ _ _ _ _ _ _

_____

_____

_ _ _ _

_____ ut

Write a sentence telling what you wore to school today.

_____

_ _

_____

_ _

_____

What is the word  _____

without  ? _ _ _ _ _ _ _ _ _ _ _

_____

Complete the sentence.

One classroom rule I should always follow is

_____

_ _ _ _ _ _ _ _ _ _ _ _ _ _ _ _ _ _

_____

_ _ _ _ _ _ _ _ _ _ _ _ _ _ _ _ _ _

_____

Draw an object that begins with the /n/ sound.

Circle each **J** and **j**.

J	y	u	j
P	O	j	k
v	B	j	N
m	k	J	i

Read each word with an adult. Circle the words with two syllables in orange. Circle the words with three syllables in blue.

enamel   **toothpaste**

cavity   **dentist**

Trace and write the letters **Nn**.

Think about a book you listened to this week. Draw your favorite part.

Write the missing letter in the color word. Color the crayon.

_____

yel ___ ow

Draw two objects whose names rhyme.

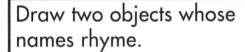

Write the sentence correctly.

didd my cup spill everywhere

Write the name of two things that you cannot live without.

_____

— — — — — — — — — — — —

_____

— — — — — — — — — — — —

_____

Draw a picture of something you did this morning.

Circle the picture whose name has two syllables.

Draw a line to connect each picture to the letter of its beginning sound.

s

l

Draw a face to show how you feel about broccoli.

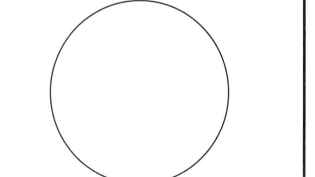

g

k

Circle the pictures that go together.

Read a fiction book with an adult. Draw a picture of one of the characters.

Read a fiction book with an adult. Write one character's name.

_____

– – – – – – – – – – –

_____

– – – – – – – – – – –

_____

_____

– – –

_____ctopus

Write a sentence telling about your favorite zoo animal.

_____

– – – – – – – – – – – – – – – – – – –

_____

– – – – – – – – – – – – – – – – – – –

_____

What is the word without ? _____

_ _ _ _ _ _ _ _ _ _ _ _ _ _ _ _ _ _ _ _

_____

Complete the sentence.

I can live without

_____

_ _ _ _ _ _ _ _ _ _ _ _ _ _ _ _

_____

_ _ _ _ _ _ _ _ _ _ _ _ _ _ _ _

_____

Draw an object that begins with the /o/ sound.

Circle each **K** and **k**.

g   h   J   k

z   L   c   K

v   B   N   m

k   I   G   t

Read each word with an adult. Circle the words with two syllables in orange. Circle the words with three syllables in green.

backyard   **dishwasher**

inside   **submarine**

Trace and write the letters **Oo**.

Think about a book you listened to this week. Draw your favorite part.

Write the missing letter in the color word. Color the crayon.

g __ een

Draw two objects whose names each have two syllables.

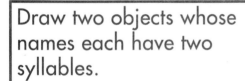

Write the sentence correctly.

ice melts and turns into water

Write the name of two things that you really want but can live without.

_____

– – – – – – – – – – – – –

_____

_____

– – – – – – – – – – – – –

_____

Draw a picture of something you ate for breakfast.

Circle the picture whose name has two syllables.

Write the letter of the beginning sound.

　　_____

　　　　　　　　　　– – – – –

　　　　　　　　　　_____

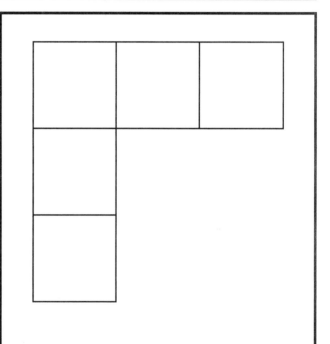

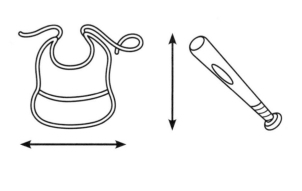

Circle the pictures that go together.

Read a fiction book with an adult. Draw a picture of one of the characters.

Read a fiction book with an adult. Write one character's name.

_____

– – – – – – – – – – – – – – – –

_____

– – – – – – – – – – – – – – – –

_____

_____

– – –

_____an

Write a sentence telling what school tools you are using to complete this page.

_____

– –

_____

_____

– –

_____

What is the word without ?

_____

— — — — — — — — — — — —

_____

Complete the sentence.

I want to go to

_____

— — — — — — — — — — — —

_____

— — — — — — — — — — — —

_____

Draw an object that begins with the /p/ sound.

Circle each **L** and **I**.

L   y   u   l

I   F   v   L

s   d   x   l

k   L   i   l

Read each word with an adult. Circle the number of syllables in each word.

helicopter	3	4
butterfly	3	4
yesterday	3	4
caterpillar	3	4

Trace and write the letters **Pp**.

P p P p

Think about a book you listened to this week. Draw your favorite part.

Write the missing letter in the color word. Color the crayon.

or _____ nge

Draw two objects whose names each have two syllables.

Write the sentence correctly.

yesterday wuz a very long day

Write a sentence telling how you feel about dessert.

_____

‒ ‒ ‒ ‒ ‒ ‒ ‒ ‒ ‒ ‒ ‒ ‒ ‒ ‒ ‒

_____

_____

‒ ‒ ‒ ‒ ‒ ‒ ‒ ‒ ‒ ‒ ‒ ‒ ‒ ‒ ‒

_____

Draw a picture of something you see in winter.

Circle the picture whose name has three syllables.

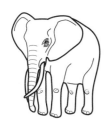 

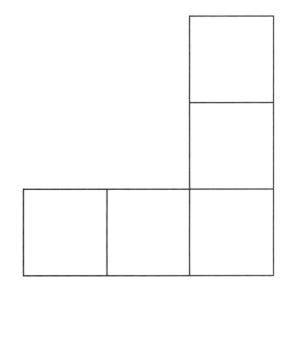

Write the letter of the beginning sound.

_____

‒ ‒ ‒

_____

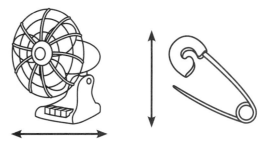

Circle the pictures that go together.

Read a fiction book with an adult. Draw a picture of one of the characters.

Read a fiction book with an adult. Write one character's name.

_____

‒ ‒ ‒ ‒ ‒ ‒ ‒ ‒ ‒ ‒ ‒ ‒ ‒

_____

_____

‒ ‒ ‒ ‒ ‒ ‒ ‒ ‒ ‒ ‒ ‒ ‒ ‒

_____

_____
‒ ‒ ‒ ‒
_____ ueen

Write a sentence telling about the animals you might see on a farm.

_____

‒ ‒ ‒ ‒ ‒ ‒ ‒ ‒ ‒ ‒ ‒ ‒ ‒ ‒ ‒ ‒ ‒ ‒ ‒ ‒

_____

_____

‒ ‒ ‒ ‒ ‒ ‒ ‒ ‒ ‒ ‒ ‒ ‒ ‒ ‒ ‒ ‒ ‒ ‒ ‒ ‒

_____

What is the word without ⬭ ?

_____

‒ ‒ ‒ ‒ ‒ ‒ ‒ ‒ ‒ ‒ ‒

_____

Complete the sentence. Draw a picture.

In winter, I like to

_____

‒ ‒ ‒ ‒ ‒ ‒ ‒ ‒ ‒ ‒

_____

Draw an object that begins with the letter q (/k w / sound).

Read each word with an adult. Circle the number of syllables in each word.

umbrella	3	4
impossible	3	4
discovery	3	4
basketball	3	4

Circle each **M** and **m**.

M	y	u	m
i	O	p	l
g	h	J	m
z	L	c	M

Trace and write the letters **Qq**.

Think about a book you listened to this week. Draw your favorite part.

Write the missing letter in the color word. Color the crayon.

pu ____ ple

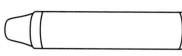

Draw two objects whose names each have two syllables.

Write the sentence correctly.

how ar we going to get there

Write a word to describe the shoes on your feet. Draw your shoes.

_____

— — — — — — — — — — — — — —

_____

Draw a picture of something you hear in winter.

Circle the picture whose name has three syllables.

Circle the letter of the ending sound.

b

m

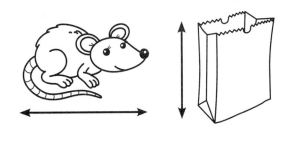

Circle the pictures that go together.

Read a fiction book with an adult. Draw a picture of one of the characters.

Read a fiction book with an adult. Write one character's name.

_____

— — — — — — — — — — — —

_____

— — — — — — — — — — — —

_____

_____

— — —

_____at

Write a sentence telling what you wear to go outside in winter.

_____

— — — — — — — — — — — —

_____

— — — — — — — — — — — —

_____

What is the word

without _____ ?

_____

— — — — — — — — — — — —

_____

Complete the sentence. Draw a picture.

In winter, I hear

_____

— — — — — — — — — — — —

_____

Draw an object that begins with the /r/ sound.

Circle each **N** and **n**.

N   y   u   n

i   N   p   l

g   h   J   n

m   k   A   n

Read each word with an adult. Circle the number of syllables in each word.

computer	3	4
alligator	3	4
potato	3	4
television	3	4

Trace and write the letters **Rr**.

RrRr - - - - - - - - - - - - - - - - - - -

Think about a book you listened to this week. Draw your favorite part.

Write the missing letter in the color word. Color the crayon.

_____

_ _ _

____lack

Draw two objects whose names each have three syllables.

Write the sentence correctly.

are wee on the winning team

Write words to describe how snow feels.

_____

– – – – – – – – – – – – – – –

_____

– – – – – – – – – – – – – – –

_____

Draw a picture of something you taste in winter.

Circle the picture whose name has three syllables.

Circle the letter of the ending sound.

s

c

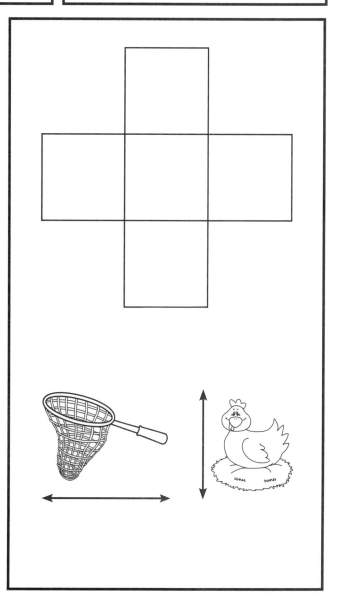

Circle the pictures that go together.

Read a fiction book with an adult. Draw a picture of one of the characters.

Read a fiction book with an adult. Write one character's name.

_____

– – – – – – – – – – – – – – – – – –

_____

– – – – – – – – – – – – – – – – – –

_____

_____
– – – –
_____nake

Write a sentence telling about your favorite ocean animal.

_____

– – – – – – – – – – – – – – – – – –

_____

– – – – – – – – – – – – – – – – – –

_____

What is the word

without  ?

_____

– – – – – – – – – – – – – – – –

_____

Complete the sentence. Draw a picture.

In winter, I taste

_____

– – – – – – – – – – – – – – – –

_____

Draw an object that begins with the /s/ sound.

Circle each **O** and **o**.

f   O   J   o

o   L   c   n

v   B   o   N

m   k   O   z

Read each word with an adult. Circle the number of syllables in each word.

dinosaur	3	4
kindergarten	3	4
dandelion	3	4
tricycle	3	4

Trace and write the letters **Ss**.

Ss Ss

Think about a book you read this week. Draw your favorite part.

Write the missing letter in the color word. Color the crayon.

_____

pi ____ k

Draw two objects whose names each have three syllables.

Write the sentence correctly.

i am excited to go tu the beach

_____

_____

_____

_____

_____

_____

_____

Write a sentence telling how you get to school.

_____

_____

_____

Draw a picture of something you smell in winter.

Circle the picture whose name has three syllables.

Circle the letter of the ending sound.

n

r

Circle the pictures that go together.

Read a fiction book with an adult. Draw a picture of one of the characters.

Read a fiction book with an adult. Write one character's name.

_____

_____

_____

_____urtle

Write a sentence telling why you should not touch things that are hot.

_____

_____

_____

What is the word without ?

_____

Complete the sentence. Draw a picture.

In winter, I smell

_____

Draw an object that begins with the /t/ sound.

Circle each **P** and **p**.

Q	w	P	e
p	r	T	s
P	y	u	p
i	O	p	k

Read each word with an adult. Circle the number of syllables in each word.

grasshopper	3	4
macaroni	3	4
camera	3	4
cooperate	3	4

Trace and write the letters **Tt**.

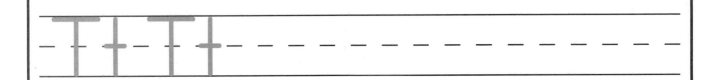

Think about a book you read this week. Draw your favorite part.

Write the missing letter in the color word.

whi ____ e

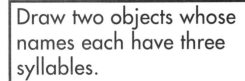

Draw two objects whose names each have three syllables.

Write the sentence correctly.

can we go eet lunch now

_____

_____

_____

_____

Write a sentence telling about your favorite activity.

_____

_____

_____

Draw a picture of something you do in winter.

Circle the picture whose name has four syllables.

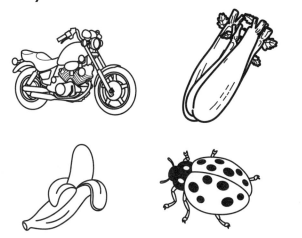

Circle the letter of the ending sound.

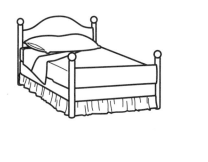

d

g

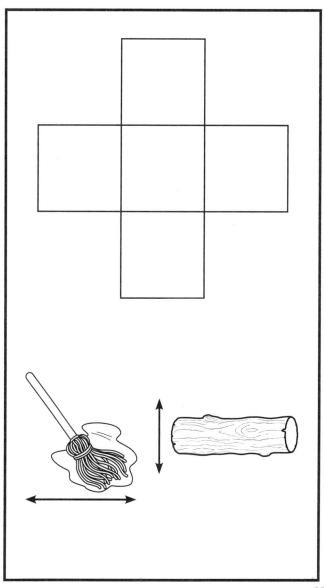

Circle the pictures that go together.

Read a fiction book with an adult. Draw a picture of one of the characters.

Read a fiction book with an adult. Write one character's name.

_____

_____

_____

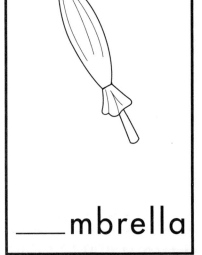

___mbrella

Write a sentence about your favorite insect.

_____

_____

_____

What is the word
without the /t/ sound?

_____

Complete the sentence. Draw a picture.

In winter, I do not like to

_____

Draw an object that begins with the /u/ sound.

Circle each **Q** and **q**.

a	q	F	v
Q	s	d	x
q	B	N	m
Q	k	A	L

Draw a line to match each pair of opposites.

happy	**girl**
up	**sad**
boy	**down**

Trace and write the letters **Uu**.

Uu Uu - - - - - - - - - - - - - - - -

Think about a book you read this week. Draw your favorite part.

Write the missing letter in the color word. Color the crayon.

bro____n

Draw two objects whose names each have four syllables.

Write the sentence correctly.

i wint to the library today

_____

_____

_____

_____

Write a sentence about your favorite thing to eat for dinner.

_____

_____

_____

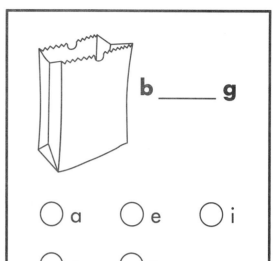

b _____ g

○ a   ○ e   ○ i

○ o   ○ u

Circle the picture whose name has four syllables.

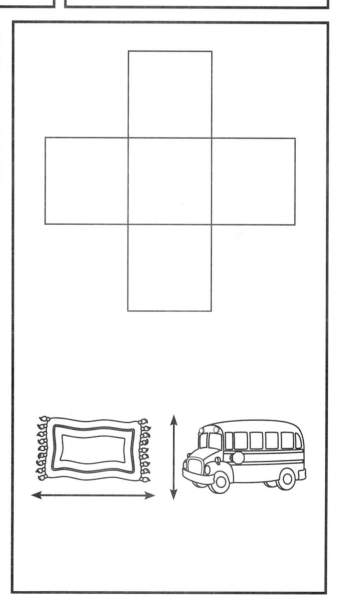

Circle the letter of the ending sound.

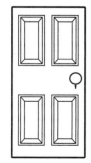

g

r

Read a fiction book with an adult. Draw a picture of the setting.

Which word is an adjective?

○ **pickle**

○ **loud**

○ **bear**

Read a fiction book with an adult. Write one sentence about the setting.

_____

_____

_____

_____ a n

Think of an adjective to describe thunder. Use it in a sentence.

_____

_____

_____

What is the word

without the /p/ sound?

_____

Make a list of three adjectives to describe how you feel today. Draw a face to show how you feel.

_____

_____

_____

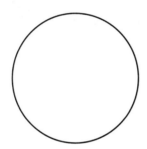

Draw an object that begins with the /v/ sound.

Circle each **R** and **r**.

A   w   R   e

r   q   B   T

R   y   u   r

i   r   D   I

Draw a line to match each pair of opposites.

hot   small

awake   cold

big   asleep

Trace and write the letters **Vv**.

Think about a book you read this week. Draw your favorite part.

Circle the letter of the ending sound.

b   d

Draw two objects whose names each have four syllables.

Write about your favorite part of a book you read this week.

_____

_____

_____

_____

Write a sentence about wind.

_____

_____

_____

p _____ n

◯ a   ◯ e   ◯ i

◯ o   ◯ u

Circle the picture whose name has four syllables.

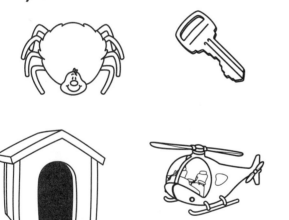

Draw a straight line through the letters of the word **can**.

d	c	n
c	a	n
h	s	f

Write the word.

_____

Circle the letter of the ending sound.

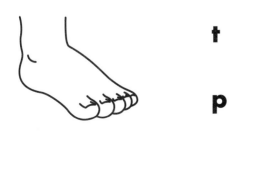

t

p

Read a fiction book with an adult.
Draw a picture of the setting.

Which word is an adjective?

○ **key**

○ **foot**

○ **smelly**

Read a fiction book with an adult. Write one
sentence about the setting.

_____

_____

_____

_____ig

Draw a picture of something that is smelly.

What is the word 🐁
without the /r/ sound?

_____

Make a list of three adjectives to describe your home. Draw a picture.

_____

_____

Draw an object that begins with the /w/ sound.

Circle each **S** and **s**.

g   h   J   s

z   L   c   S

s   B   N   m

S   k   A   s

Draw a line to match each pair of opposites.

tall   **wrong**

correct   **mean**

nice   **short**

Trace and write the letters **Ww**.

Think about a book you read this week. Draw your favorite part.

Circle the letter of the ending sound.

k   x

Draw two objects whose names each have four syllables.

Write about your favorite part of a book you read this week.

_____

_____

_____

_____

_____

Write a sentence about a party.

_____

_____

_____

 f____ sh

◯ a   ◯ e   ◯ i

◯ o   ◯ u

Circle the picture whose name has four syllables.

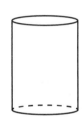

Draw a straight line through the letters of the word **how**.

p	l	y
h	j	k
h	o	w

Circle the letter of the ending sound.

k

l

Write the word.

_____

Read a fiction book with an adult.
Draw a picture of the setting.

Which word is an adjective?

○ **cookie**

○ **bowl**

○ **hard**

Read a fiction book with an adult. Write one
sentence about the setting.

_____

_____

_____

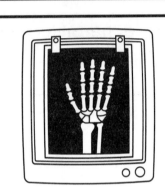

_____–ray

Think of an adjective to describe a rock. Use the word in a sentence.

_____

_____

_____

What is the word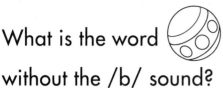
without the /b/ sound?

_____

Make a list of three adjectives to describe your bedroom. Draw a picture.

_____

_____

_____

Draw an object that begins with the letter **x**.

Circle each **T** and **t**.

T   y   u   t

i   O   D   l

t   B   N   m

T   k   o   t

Draw a line to match each pair of opposites.

dark   night

day   wet

dry   light

Trace and write the letters **Xx**.

Think about a book you read this week. Draw your favorite part.

Circle the letter of the ending sound.

t   d

Which sight word rhymes with ?

○ **is**

○ **at**

○ **of**

Write about your favorite part of a book you read this week.

_____

_____

_____

_____

_____

Write a sentence about your classroom.

_____

_____

_____

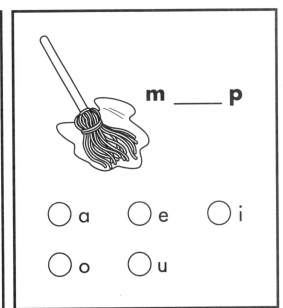

m ____ p

◯ a   ◯ e   ◯ i

◯ o   ◯ u

Read the word. Add the letter **e** to the end of the word. Draw a picture to match the new word.

kit

kit + e = _____

Draw a straight line through the letters of the word **the**.

t	c	n
c	h	n
h	n	e

Write the word.

_____

Circle the letter of the ending sound.

t

f

Read a fiction book with an adult.
Draw a picture of the setting.

Which word is an adjective?

○ **fox**

○ **quiet**

○ **leaf**

Read a fiction book with an adult. Write a
sentence about the setting.

_____

_____

_____

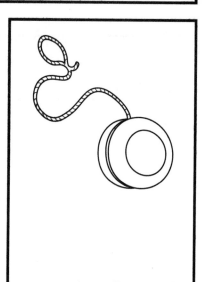

_____o-yo

Draw a picture of yourself doing something quiet.

What is the word

without the /h/ sound?

_____

Make a list of three adjectives to describe a family car. Draw a picture.

_____

_____

_____

Draw an object that begins with the /y/ sound.

Circle each **U** and **u**.

U   h   J   u

z   L   c   U

u   B   N   m

U   k   e   A

Draw a line to match each pair of opposites.

early   **hard**

easy   **late**

full   **empty**

Trace and write the letters **Yy**.

Think about a book you read this week. Draw your favorite part.

Circle the letter of the ending sound.

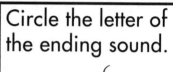

d   **g**

Which sight word rhymes with ?

○ **some**

○ **that**

○ **my**

Write about your favorite part of a book that you read this week.

_____

_____

_____

_____

Write a sentence about your favorite fruit.

_____

_____

_____

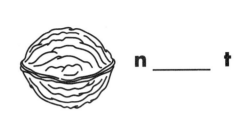

n _____ t

◯ a   ◯ e   ◯ i

◯ o   ◯ u

Read the word. Add the letter **e** to the end of the word. Draw a picture to match the new word.

can

can + e = _____

Circle the letter of the ending sound.

d

f

Draw a straight line through the letters of the word **you**.

y	o	u
j	m	k
w	o	t

Write the word.

_____

117

Read a fiction book with an adult.
Draw a picture of the setting.

Which word is an adjective?

◯ **run**

◯ **sting**

◯ **hot**

Read a fiction book with an adult. Write a
sentence about the setting.

_____

_____

_____

_____**ebra**

Think of an adjective that describes fire. Use it in a sentence.

_____

_____

_____

What is the word

without the /s/ sound?

_____

Make a list of three adjectives to describe a favorite toy. Draw a picture.

_____

_____

_____

Draw an object that begins with the /z/ sound.

Circle each **V** and **v**.

g   h   J   v

z   L   c   V

v   B   N   m

V   d   A   U

Draw a line to match each pair of opposites.

enter   true

light   heavy

false   exit

Trace and write the letters **Zz**.

ZzZz

Think about a book you read this week. Draw your favorite part.

Circle the letter of the ending sound.

t   d

Which sight word rhymes with  ?

○ **than**

○ **have**

○ **like**

Write about your favorite part in a book that you read this week.

_____

_____

_____

_____

_____

Write a sentence about a car.

_____

_____

_____

c _____ b

○ a   ○ e   ○ i

○ o   ○ u

Read the word. Add the letter **e** to the end of the word. Draw a picture to match the new word.

cap

cap + e = _____

Draw a straight line through the letters of the word **are**.

g	b	h
a	r	e
m	o	i

Write the word.

_____

Sort the words.

kit   kite   can   cane

Short Vowels	Long Vowels

Read a fiction book with an adult. Draw a picture of the setting.

Which word is an adjective?

○ **fly**

○ **pen**

○ **slow**

Read a fiction book with an adult. Write a sentence about the setting.

_____

_____

_____

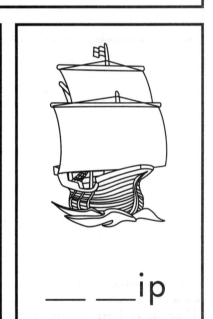

__ __ip

Draw a picture of an animal that is slow.

What is the word without the /f/ sound?

_____

Make a list of three adjectives to describe your favorite food. Draw a picture.

_____

_____

_____

Draw an object that begins with the /sh/ sound.

Circle each **W** and **w**.

W   y   u   w

I   f   z   W

w   B   N   m

W   k   o   P

Draw a line to match each pair of opposites.

fast   **slow**

near   **right**

left   **far**

Complete the sentence by circling the correct sight word.

at   can   how   I

_____ can sing!

Think about a book you read this week. Draw your favorite part.

Circle the letter of the ending sound.

g   b

Which sight word rhymes with ?

○ **be**

○ **will**

○ **what**

Write about your favorite part of a book that you read this week.

_____

_____

_____

_____

_____

Write a sentence about a flower.

_____

_____

_____

d _____ g

○ a   ○ e   ○ i

○ o   ○ u

Read the word. Add the letter **e** to the end of the word. Draw a picture to match the new word.

pin

pin + e = _____

Sort the words.

cap   cape   fin   fine

Short Vowels	Long Vowels

Draw a straight line through the letters of the word **see**.

b	h	u
h	f	p
s	e	e

Write the word.

_____

Read a fiction book with an adult. Draw a picture of the setting.

Which word is an adjective?

◯ **read**

◯ **smooth**

◯ **crab**

Read a fiction book with an adult. Write a sentence about the setting.

_____

_____

_____

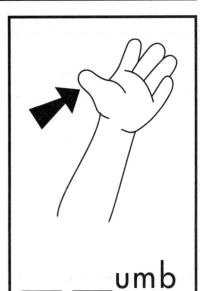

___ ___umb

Think about an adjective that describes glass. Use it in a sentence.

_____

_____

_____

What is the word

without the /s/ sound?

_____

Make a list of three adjectives to describe your favorite game. Draw a picture

_____

_____

Draw an object that begins with the /th/ sound.

Circle each **X** and **x**.

A   w   X   e

q   x   R   D

X   y   u   x

H   x   Y   e

Draw a line to match each pair of opposites.

first   **sink**

float   **found**

lost   **last**

Complete the sentence by circling the correct sight word.

is   **me**   **you**   **be**

Will you go with _____?

Think about a book you read this week. Draw your favorite part.

Circle the letter of the ending sound.

h   **x**

Which sight word rhymes with  ?

○ **with**

○ **little**

○ **said**

Write about our favorite part of a book that you read this week.

_____

_____

_____

_____

_____

Write a sentence about what you like to do in art class.

_____

_____

_____

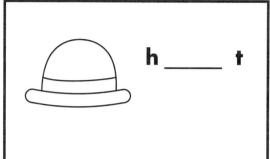 **h** ____ **t**

◯ a   ◯ e   ◯ i

◯ o   ◯ u

Read each word. Add the letter **e** to the end of each word. Write each new word.

fin

_____

cub

_____

Draw a straight line through the letters of the word **and**.

a	z	x
q	n	r
w	c	d

Write the word.

_____

Sort the words.

tub   hope   tube   hop

Short Vowels	Long Vowels

Read a fiction book with an adult.
Draw a picture of the setting.

Which word is an adjective?

◯ **large**

◯ **box**

◯ **tree**

Read a fiction book with an adult. Write a
sentence about the setting.

_____

_____

_____

__ __in

Draw a picture of something large.

What is the word
without the /s/ sound?

_____

Make a list of three adjectives to describe a trip you took. Draw a picture.

_____

_____

_____

Draw an object that begins with the /ch/ sound.

Circle each **Y** and **y**.

g   h   J   y

z   L   c   Y

y   B   N   m

Y   k   d   A

Draw a line to match each pair of opposites.

soft   **take**

give   **stop**

go   **hard**

Complete the sentence by circling the correct sight word.

he   are   that   see

Is _____ going with you?

Think about a book you read this week. Draw your favorite part.

Circle the letter of the ending sound.

l   m

Which sight word rhymes with 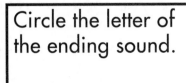 ?

○ **do**

○ **about**

○ **were**

Write about your favorite part of a book that you read this week.

_____

_____

_____

_____

_____

Write a sentence about what you like to do in PE class.

_____

_____

_____

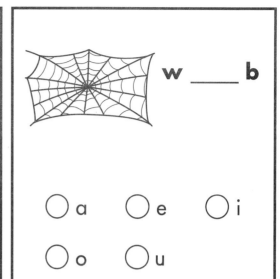

w ____ b

○ a   ○ e   ○ i

○ o   ○ u

Read each word. Add the letter **e** to the end of each word. Write each new word.

tub

_____

mad

_____

Draw a straight line through the letters of the word **did**.

d	m	b
k	i	w
a	s	d

Write the word.

_____

Sort the words.

hug   made   huge   mad

Short Vowels	Long Vowels

Read a fiction book with an adult.
Draw a picture of the setting.

Which word is an adjective?

○ **frog**

○ **jump**

○ **friendly**

Read a fiction book with an adult. Write a
sentence about the setting.

_____

_____

_____

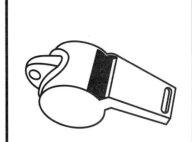

__ __istle

Think about an adjective that describes a friend. Use it in a sentence.

_____

_____

_____

What is the word

without the /p/ sound?

_____

Make a list of three adjectives to describe your favorite dessert. Draw a picture.

_____

_____

_____

Draw an object that begins with the letters **wh**.

Circle each **Z** and **z**.

A   w   Z   e

q   z   R   Z

g   h   J   t

f   L   c   Z

Draw a line to match each pair of opposites.

high   **out**

short   **low**

in   **long**

Complete the sentence by circling the correct sight word.

she   that   are   is

What is _____ bug over there?

Think about a book you read this week. Draw your favorite part.

Circle the letter of the ending sound.

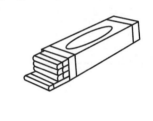

b   m

Which sight word rhymes with ?

○ **we**

○ **up**

○ **her**

Write about your favorite part of a book that you read this week.

_____

_____

_____

_____

_____

Write a sentence about rain.

_____

_____

_____

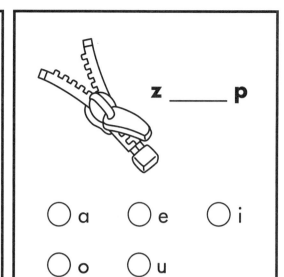

z _____ p

○ a   ○ e   ○ i

○ o   ○ u

Read each word. Add the letter **e** to the end of each word. Write each new word.

bit

_____

hop

_____

Draw a straight line through the letters of the word **for**.

t	k	m
f	o	r
x	z	p

Write the word.

_____

Sort the words.

rat   rate   mane   man

Short Vowels	Long Vowels

Read a fiction book with an adult.
Draw a picture of the setting.

Which word is a verb?

○ **smell**

○ **soft**

○ **pool**

Read a fiction book with an adult. Write a
sentence about the setting.

_____

_____

_____

___ ___one

Draw a picture of yourself smelling something.

What is the word 🐌

without the /s/ sound?

_____

Make a list of three adjectives to describe a favorite friend. Draw a picture.

_____

_____

_____

Write one sentence about a favorite friend. Use at least one adjective.

_____

_____

_____

Draw an object that begins with the letters **ph**.

Use the letters to make words. Write the words.

w   e   r   t
y   u   p

_____

_____

_____

_____

Complete the sentence by circling the correct sight word.

we   **said**   **and**   **do**

They _____ that we should all go.

Write one word in each category.

Food   Square Things

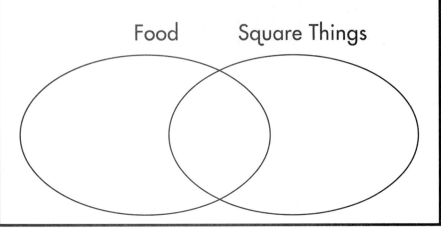

Circle the letter of the ending sound.

m   **n**

Which sight word rhymes with ?

○ **in**

○ **where**

○ **it**

Write about how two books you read this week are the same and different.

Same:_____

_____

Different:_____

_____

_____

_____

Write a sentence about something you once made.

_____

_____

_____

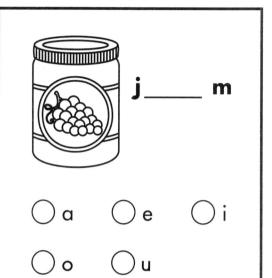

j _____ m

◯ a   ◯ e   ◯ i

◯ o   ◯ u

Read each word. Add the letter **e** to the end of each word. Write each new word.

pip

_____

rid

_____

Draw a straight line through the letters of the word **but**.

h	x	s
b	j	k
b	u	t

Write the word.

_____

Sort the words.

rag   **tap**   **tape**   **rage**

Short Vowels	Long Vowels

Read a fiction book. Draw a picture of a part at the beginning.

Which word is a verb?

○ **toy**

○ **run**

○ **wet**

Read a fiction book. Write two sentences about what happened at the beginning.

_____

_____

_____

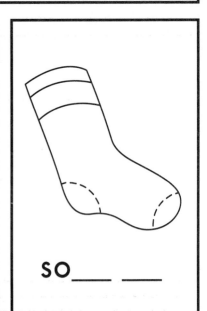

SO___ ___

Think about a verb that tells something you do in baseball. Use it in a sentence.

_____

_____

_____

Say the word **meat**. Say it without the /t/ sound. Write the new word.

_____

Make a list of three adjectives to describe a favorite teacher. Draw a picture.

_____

_____

_____

Draw an object that begins with the /s/ sound and ends with the /l/ sound.

Use the letters to make words. Write the words.

a   s   d   m
g   o   l

_____

_____

_____

_____

Write one sentence about a favorite teacher. Use at least one adjective.

_____

_____

_____

Complete the sentence by circling the correct sight word.

will   The   it   than

_____ show is about to begin.

Write one word in each category.

Animals   Things with Wings

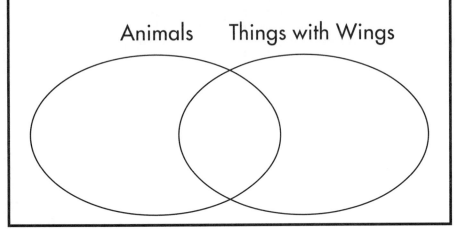

Circle the letter of the ending sound.

o   u

Which sight word rhymes with  ?

○ **make**

○ **when**

○ **they**

Write about how two books you read this week are the same and different.

Same:_____

_____

Different:_____

_____

_____

Write a sentence about your home.

_____

_____

_____

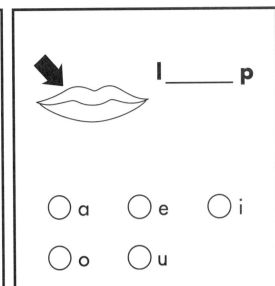

l ____ p

○ a   ○ e   ○ i

○ o   ○ u

Add the letter **e** to the word. Use the new word in a sentence.

cub + e = _____

_____

_____

Draw a straight line through the letters of the word **his**.

h	c	l
i	a	b
s	w	f

Write the word.

_____

Sort the words.

fad   fade   bit   bite

Short Vowels	Long Vowels

Read a nonfiction book. Draw a picture of something you read about.

Which word is a verb?

○ **dark**

○ **car**

○ **hop**

Read a nonfiction book. Write one thing you learned from the book.

_____

_____

_____

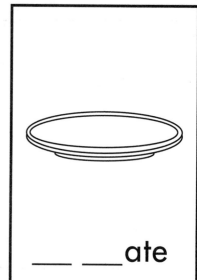

__ __ate

Draw a picture of something that hops.

Say the word **tooth**. Say it without the /th/ sound. Write the new word.

_____

Make a list of three adjectives to describe a favorite book character. Draw a picture.

_____

_____

_____

Write one sentence about your favorite book character. Use at least one adjective.

_____

_____

_____

Draw an object that begins with the /d/ sound and ends with the /r/ sound.

Use the letters to make words. Write the words.

c   i   b   n
a   k   m

_____

_____

_____

_____

_____

Complete the sentence by circling the correct sight word.

like   **did**   **my**   **but**

May I have _____ toys back?

Write one word in each category.

Food   Round Things

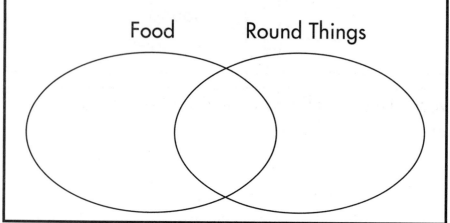

Circle the letter of the ending sound.

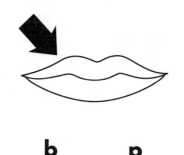

b   **p**

Which sight word rhymes with ?

○ **on**

○ **them**

○ **she**

Write about how two books you read this week are the same and different.

Same: _____

_____

Different: _____

_____

_____

Write a sentence about a trip you took.

_____

_____

_____

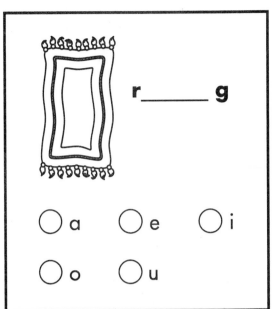

r_____ g

○ a   ○ e   ○ i

○ o   ○ u

Add the letter **e** to the word. Use the new word in a sentence.

hug + e = _____

_____

_____

Draw a straight line through the letters of the word **was**.

k	w	n
g	a	q
o	s	m

Write the word.

_____

Sort the words.

pip   ripe   pipe   rip

Short Vowels	Long Vowels

Read a book about a zoo animal. Draw a picture of something you read about.

Which word is a verb?

○ **kind**

○ **chair**

○ **skate**

Read a book about a zoo animal. Write one sentence about what you learned.

_____

_____

_____

__ __ab

Think about a verb that tells something you do on ice. Use it in a sentence.

_____

_____

_____

Say the word **boat**. Say it without the /t/ sound. Write the new word.

_____

Make a list of three adjectives to describe your favorite month. Draw a picture.

_____

_____

_____

Draw an object that begins with the /m/ sound and ends with the /t/ sound.

Write one sentence about your favorite month. Use at least one adjective.

_____

_____

_____

Use the letters to make words. Write the words.

e j d f
a   h   t

_____

_____

_____

_____

_____

Complete the sentence by circling the correct sight word.

for   have   in   little

The _____ kitten is cute.

Write one word in each category.

Loud Things   Tools

Circle the letter of the ending sound.

g   r

Which sight word rhymes with  ?

○ **no**

○ **who**

○ **this**

Write about how two books you read this week are the same and different.

Same:_____

_____

Different:_____

_____

_____

Write a sentence telling one rule you have to follow at home.

_____

_____

_____

Draw a picture of something you see in spring.

Add the letter **e** to the word. Use the new word in a sentence.

cut + e = _____

_____

_____

Sort the words.

mope   **not**   **mop**   **note**

Short Vowels	Long Vowels

Draw a straight line through the letters of the word **not**.

r	c	n
t	f	o
q	w	t

Write the word.

_____

Read a book about an ocean animal. Draw a picture of something you read about.

Which word is a verb?

○ **color**

○ **pen**

○ **paper**

Read a book about an ocean animal. Write one sentence about what you learned.

_____

_____

_____

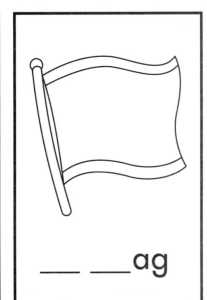

__ __ag

Draw a picture of something you like to color. Color it.

Say the word **pipe**. Say it without the ending /p/ sound. Write the new word.

_____

Make a list of three adjectives to describe your favorite day. Draw a picture.

_____

_____

_____

Draw an object that begins with the /p/ sound and ends with the /l/ sound.

Use the letters to make words. Write the words.

w s b e
d n i

_____

_____

_____

_____

_____

Write one sentence about your favorite day. Use at least one adjective.

_____

_____

_____

Complete the sentence by circling the correct sight word.

up   **what**   **each**   **where**

I will give _____ of you a sticker.

Write one word in each category.

School Tools   Can Roll

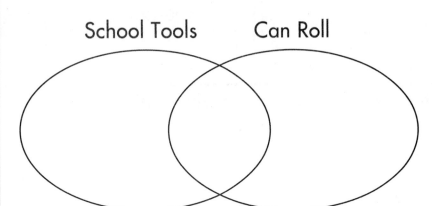

Circle the letter of the ending sound.

s   f

Which sight word rhymes with ?

○ **if**

○ **there**

○ **other**

Write about how two books you read this week are the same and different.

Same:_____

_____

Different:_____

_____

_____

Write a sentence about your favorite holiday.

_____

_____

_____

Draw a picture of something you hear in spring.

Add the letter **s** to make the word plural. Draw a picture to match the new word.

star + s = _____

Draw a straight line through the letters of the word **has**.

h	i	x
g	a	n
p	m	s

Write the word.

_____

Which is the correct plural form of the word **apple**?

○ **apples**

○ **applies**

○ **appls**

Read a book about insects. Draw a picture of something you read about.

Which word is a verb?

◯ **tiny**

◯ **swim**

◯ **sunshine**

Read a book about insects. Write one sentence about what you learned.

_____

_____

_____

___ ___esent

Think about a verb that tells something you do in water. Use it in a sentence.

_____

_____

_____

Replace the first sound in **man** with the /p/ sound to make a new word. Write the new word.

_____

Use at least three of the sight words in a sentence.

**has   been   him   this
who   had   other**

_____

_____

_____

_____

Draw an object that begins with the /n/ sound and ends with the /t/ sound.

Use the letters to make words. Write the words.

**a   r   c   y
f   o   m**

_____

_____

_____

_____

_____

Complete the spelling pyramid for the word **some**.

— —

— — — —

— — — — — —

— — — — — — — —

Complete the sentence by circling the correct sight word.

she   **more**   **on**   **was**

I want _____ rice, please.

Write one word in each category.

Clothes   Can Get Wet

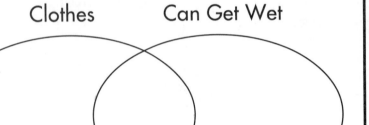

Circle the letter of the ending sound.

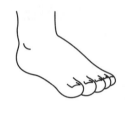

d   **t**

Which sight word rhymes with ?

○ **as**

○ **then**

○ **into**

Write about how two books you read this week are the same and different.

Same: _____

_____

Different: _____

_____

_____

Write a sentence about a visit to the dentist.

_____

_____

_____

Draw a picture of something you taste in spring.

Add the letter **s** to make the word plural. Draw a picture to match the new word.

bat + s = _____

Draw a straight line through the letters of the word **all**.

a	l	l
z	j	y
m	k	d

Write the word.

_____

Which is the correct plural form of the word **day**?

○ **dayes**

○ **days**

○ **daes**

Read a book about families. Draw a picture showing one thing you learned.

Which word is a verb?

○ **bubbly**

○ **dad**

○ **hug**

Read a book about families. Write one sentence about what you learned.

_____

_____

_____

__ __ar

Draw a picture of someone or something you like to hug.

Replace the first sound in **house** with the /m/ sound to make a new word. Write the new word.

_____

Use at least three of the sight words in a sentence.

about	**then**	**of**	**as**
were	**into**	**one**	

_____

_____

_____

_____

Draw an object that begins with the /j/ sound and ends with the /r/ sound.

Use the letters to make words. Write the words.

o h p x
a b t

_____

_____

_____

_____

_____

_____

Complete the spelling pyramid for the word **like**.

___

___ ___

___ ___ ___

___ ___ ___ ___

Complete the sentence by circling the correct sight word.

her   make   his   all

Let's _____ a cake for your sister.

Write one word in each category.

Bug   Can Fly

Circle the letter of the ending sound.

4

n   r

Which sight word rhymes with [🚪] ?

○ **your**

○ **one**

○ **which**

Write about how two books you read this week are the same and different.

Same:_____

_____

Different:_____

_____

_____

_____

Write a sentence about a farm.

_____

_____

_____

Draw a picture of something you smell in spring.

Add the letter **s** to make the word plural. Draw a picture to match the new word.

log + s = _____

Draw a straight line through the letters of the word **him**.

t	y	s
h	i	m
q	c	j

Write the word.

_____

Which is the correct plural form of the word **lion**?

◯ **liones**

◯ **lionies**

◯ **lions**

Read a book about outer space. Draw a picture showing something you learned.

Which word is a verb?

○ **mouth**

○ **book**

○ **whisper**

Read a book about outer space. Write one sentence about what you learned.

_____

_____

_____

___ ___ee

Think about a verb that tells something you do in a library. Use it in a sentence.

_____

_____

_____

Replace the first sound in **fish** with the /d/ sound to make a new word. Write the new word.

_____

Use at least three of the sight words in a sentence.

**am   which   to   out
your   there   by**

_____

_____

_____

_____

Complete the spelling pyramid for the word **with**.

____

____ ____

____ ____ ____

____ ____ ____ ____

Draw an object that begins with the /p/ sound and ends with the /r/ sound.

Use the letters to make words. Write the words.

**u   t   c   g
e   l   k**

_____

_____

_____

_____

_____

Complete the sentence by circling the correct sight word.

When   **No**   **Not**   **Would**

_____ you mind helping me clean up?

Write one word in each category.

Things in the Sky   Gives Light

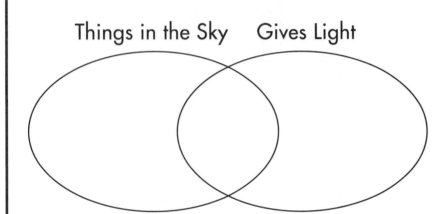

Circle the letter of the ending sound.

h   **g**

Which sight word rhymes with ?

◯ **out**

◯ **been**

◯ **so**

Write about how two books you read this week are the same and different.

Same:_____

_____

Different:_____

_____

_____

Write a sentence about a city.

_____

_____

_____

Draw a picture of something you do in spring.

Add the letter **s** to make the word plural. Draw a picture to match the new word.

rug + s = _____

Draw a straight line through the letters of the word **had**.

i	c	d
f	a	s
h	b	e

Write the word.

_____

Which is the correct plural form of the word **cloud**?

◯ **clouds**

◯ **cloudes**

◯ **cloudss**

Read a book about a community helper. Draw a picture showing one thing you learned.

Which word is a verb?

○ **spell**

○ **team**

○ **happy**

Read a book about a community helper. Write one sentence about what you learned.

_____

_____

_____

__ __og

Write a word that you are learning to spell in large letters below. Use crayons to trace each letter in a different color.

Replace the first sound in **hive** with the /f/ sound to make a new word. Write the new word.

_____

Use at least three of the sight words in a sentence.

an   these   why   the
some   at   can

_____

_____

_____

_____

Draw an object that begins with the /b/ sound and ends with the /g/ sound.

Use the letters to make words. Write the words.

w   e   r   t
a   s   d

_____

_____

_____

_____

_____

Complete the spelling pyramid for the word **said**.

—

— —

— — —

— — — —

Complete the sentence by circling the correct sight word.

them   **if**   **many**   **or**

We will go swimming _____ it does not rain.

Compare and contrast two books you read this week.

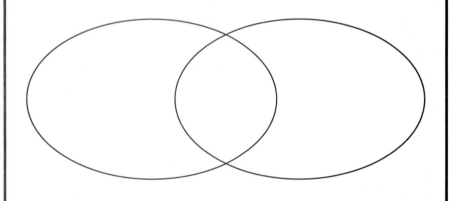

Circle the letter of the ending sound.

x   **l**

Which sight word rhymes with ?

◯ **from**

◯ **these**

◯ **by**

Write about how two books you read this week are the same and different.

Same:_____

_____

Different:_____

_____

_____

Write a sentence telling your favorite thing about kindergarten.

_____

_____

_____

Draw a picture showing how you feel during the last week of school.

Add the letter **s** to make the word plural. Draw a picture to match the new word.

jar + s = _____

Draw a straight line through the letters of the word **why**.

z	c	y
e	h	g
w	n	f

Write the word.

_____

Which is the correct plural form of the word **pencil**?

⭕ **pencilies**

⭕ **pencils**

⭕ **penciles**

Read a book about friendship. Draw a picture showing one thing you learned.

Which word is a verb?

○ **think**

○ **nose**

○ **eyes**

Read a book about friendship. Write one sentence about what you learned.

_____

_____

_____

__ __own

Think about a verb that tells something you do when you are using your brain to read and do math. Use it in a sentence.

_____

_____

_____

Replace the first sound in **pig** with the /w/ sound to make a new word. Write the new word.

_____

Use at least three of the sight words in a sentence.

can   are   see   and
did   for   all

_____

_____

_____

_____

Draw an object that begins with the /d/ sound and ends with the /l/ sound.

Use the letters to make words. Write the words.

f g o l
i k m e

_____

_____

_____

_____

_____

Complete the spelling pyramid for the word **your**.

____

____ ____ ____

____ ____ ____ ____

Complete the sentence by circling the correct sight word.

they   **so**   **with**   **from**

There is a gift _____ your grandparents on the table.

Compare and contrast two books you read this week.

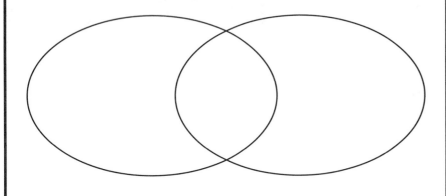

Circle the letter of the ending sound.

r   **n**

Which sight word rhymes with ?

○ **or**

○ **am**

○ **to**

Write about how two books you read this week are the same and different.

Same:_____

_____

Different:_____

_____

_____

are	be	by	find
and	away	but	down
all	at	blue	come
a	as	big	can

go	funny	from	for
help	he	have	had
in	I	his	here
little	jump	it	is

my	one	run	the
me	on	red	that
make	of	play	see
look	not	or	said

to	we	when	you
three	was	where	yellow
this	up	what	words
they	two	were	with

Answer Key

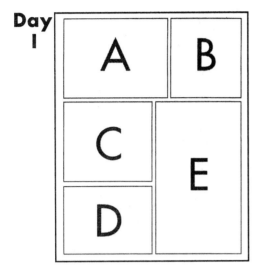

Day 1

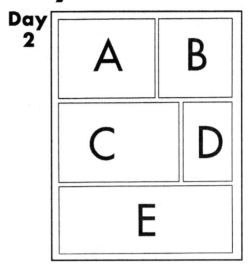

Day 2

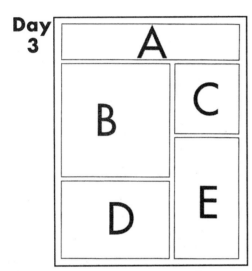

Day 3

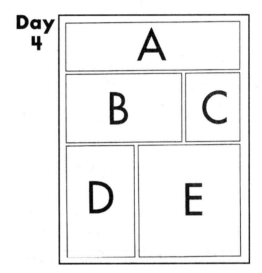

Day 4

Week 1, Day 1 (page 17)

A–C. Answers will vary.
D. cat, bat, hat, rat; E. Check students' sorting.

Week 1, Day 2 (page 18)

A. banana; B. Answers will vary.
C. Check students' sorting; D. a;
E. can, man, pan

Week 1, Day 3 (page 19)

A. Answers will vary. B. pencil, book, chair, flag; C. Answers will vary. D. Check students' sorting; E. mug, pan

Week 1, Day 4 (page 20)

A. Check students' handwriting;
B. Check students' sorting.
C. Answers will vary. D. lip, sap;
E. Answers will vary.

Week 2, Day 1 (page 21)

A–B. Answers will vary. C. Check students' matches; D. tree, bee, key; E. Check students' sorting.

Week 2, Day 2 (page 22)

A. snowman; B–C. Answers will vary. D. b; E. pie, tie, fly, cry

Answer Key

Week 2, Day 3 (page 23)

A. Check students' handwriting;
B. apple, strawberry, stop sign;
C. Answers will vary. D. circled in
red: ball, cab; circled in blue: belly,
candy; E. bug, sit, fog, hug

Week 2, Day 4 (page 24)

A. Check students' handwriting;
B. Answers will vary. C. 4; D. pop,
bin, sag, log; E. Answers will vary.

Week 3, Day 1 (page 25)

A–B. Answers will vary. C. Check
students' matches; D. glue, shoe,
two; E. Check students' sorting.

Week 3, Day 2 (page 26)

A. hedgehog; B–C. Answers will
vary. D. c; E. cake, rake, snowflake,
lake, snake

Week 3, Day 3 (page 27)

A. Check students' handwriting;
B. blueberries, first prize ribbon;
C. Answers will vary. D. circled
in red: dog, mop; circled in blue:
tiger, basket; E. fox, wig, jug, dog

Week 3, Day 4 (page 28)

A. Check students' handwriting;
B. Answers will vary. C. 4; D. lad,
bus, car, tub; E. Answers will vary.

Week 4, Day 1 (page 29)

A–B. Answers will vary. C. Check
students' matches; D. sock, clock,
rock, block; E. Check students'
sorting.

Week 4, Day 2 (page 30)

A. apple; B–C. Answers will vary.
D. d; E. dice, ice, mice

Week 4, Day 3 (page 31)

A. Check students' handwriting;
B. corn, banana, sun; C. Answers
will vary. D. circled in yellow: frog,
ball; circled in green: baby, robot;
E. get, shoe, bob

Week 4, Day 4 (page 32)

A. Check students' handwriting;
B. Answers will vary. C. 4; D. chair,
mouse, bee, cot; E. Answers will
vary.

Week 5, Day 1 (page 33)

A–B. Answers will vary. C. Check
students' matching; D. dog, log;
E. bird/b, sock/s, two/t

Week 5, Day 2 (page 34)

A. broccoli; B–C. Answers will vary.
D. e; E. Answers will vary.

Week 5, Day 3 (page 35)

A. Check students' handwriting;
B. frog, turtle, broccoli; C. Answers
will vary. D. circled in yellow: boat,
dish; circled in green: driveway,
garage; E. Check students' circling.

Week 5, Day 4 (page 36)

A. Check students' handwriting;
B. Answers will vary. C. 4;
D–E. Answers will vary.

Answer Key

Week 6, Day 1 (page 37)

A–B. Answers will vary. C. Check students' matching; D. mop, top; E. fan/f, bow/b, mat/m

Week 6, Day 2 (page 38)

A. valentine heart; B–C. Answers will vary. D. f; E. Answers will vary.

Week 6, Day 3 (page 39)

A. Check students' handwriting; B. pumpkin, carrot, orange; C. Answers will vary. D. circled in orange: door, chair; circled in purple: window, table; E. Check students' circling.

Week 6, Day 4 (page 40)

A. Check students' handwriting; B. Answers will vary. C. 5; D. Answers will vary. E. The ball is red.

Week 7, Day 1 (page 41)

A–B. Answers will vary. C. Check students' matching; D. hat, cat; E. fish/f, van/v, hen/h

Week 7, Day 2 (page 42)

A. raspberry, fly; B–C. Answers will vary. D. g; E. Answers will vary.

Week 7, Day 3 (page 43)

A. Check students' handwriting; B. grapes, eggplant, jam; C. Answers will vary. D. circled in orange: rain, sad; circled in purple: happy, sunshine; E. Check students' circling.

Week 7, Day 4 (page 44)

A. Check students' handwriting; B. Answers will vary. C. 5; D. Answers will vary. E. The blue car is fast.

Week 8, Day 1 (page 45)

A–B. Answers will vary. C. Check students' matching; D. van, fan; E. door/d, nut/n, pig/p

Week 8, Day 2 (page 46)

A. crab, book; B–C. Answers will vary. D. h; E. Answers will vary.

Week 8, Day 3 (page 47)

A. Check students' handwriting; B. pretzel, bag, football, bear; C. Answers will vary. D. circled in brown: surprise, asleep; circled in black: potato, hospital; E. Check students' circling.

Week 8, Day 4 (page 48)

A. Check students' handwriting; B. Answers will vary. C. 4; D. Answers will vary. E. The bird is yellow.

Week 9, Day 1 (page 49)

A–B. Answers will vary. C. ball; D. Answers will vary. E. mop/m, cat/c, bat/b

Week 9, Day 2 (page 50)

A. money, TV; B–C. Answers will vary. D. i; E. Answers will vary.

Answer Key

Week 9, Day 3 (page 51)

A. Check students' handwriting;
B. ant, bat, penguin, top hat;
C. Answers will vary. D. circled in brown: grandpa, address; circled in black: apricot, piano; E. Check students' circling.

Week 9, Day 4 (page 52)

A. Check students' handwriting;
B. Answers will vary. C. 7;
D. Answers will vary. E. A green frog hopped on me.

Week 10, Day 1 (page 53)

A–B. Answers will vary. C. cat;
D. Answers will vary. E. sun/s, fish/f, hat/h

Week 10, Day 2 (page 54)

A. bug, plate; B. Answers will vary.
C. Answers will vary. D. j;
E. Answers will vary.

Week 10, Day 3 (page 55)

A. Check students' handwriting;
B. lips, flamingo, pig; C. Answers will vary. D. circled in red: frozen, airplane; circled in blue: fingernail, spaghetti; E. Check students' circling.

Week 10, Day 4 (page 56)

A. Check students' handwriting;
B. Answers will vary. C. 5;
D. Answers will vary. E. The orange dripped on me.

Week 11, Day 1 (page 57)

A–B. Answers will vary. C. dog;
D. Answers will vary. E. zipper/z, violin/v, nut/n

Week 11, Day 2 (page 58)

A. porcupine, tennis racket;
B–C. Answers will vary. D. k;
E. Answers will vary.

Week 11, Day 3 (page 59)

A. Check students' handwriting;
B. snowman, egg, milk, polar bear;
C. Answers will vary. D. circled in yellow: spelling, apple; circled in green: library, officer; E. Check students' circling.

Week 11, Day 4 (page 60)

A. Check students' handwriting;
B. Answers will vary. C. 6;
D. Answers will vary. E. A purple sock is missing.

Week 12, Day 1 (page 61)

A. Check students' handwriting. B. Answers will vary. C. boat, lamp; D. Answers will vary.
E. dog/d, ball/b, goat/g

Week 12, Day 2 (page 62)

A. circle, square, triangle, rectangle; B–C. Answers will vary.
D. l; E. Answers will vary.

Answer Key

Week 12, Day 3 (page 63)

A. rain; B–C. Answers will vary.
D. circled in orange: scissors, skateboard; circled in purple: bicycle, strawberry; E. Check students' circling.

Week 12, Day 4 (page 64)

A. Check students' handwriting;
B. Answers will vary. C. r;
D. Answers will vary. E. Is my hair dark brown?

Week 13, Day 1 (page 65)

A–B. Answers will vary.
C. toothbrush; D. Answers will vary.
E. wind/w, leg/l, pan/p

Week 13, Day 2 (page 66)

A. house, building, castle;
B–C. Answers will vary. D. m;
E. Answers will vary.

Week 13, Day 3 (page 67)

A. fly; B–C. Answers will vary.
D. circled in brown: pumpkin, paper; circled in black: broccoli, cucumber; E. Check students' circling.

Week 13, Day 4 (page 68)

A. Check students' handwriting;
B. Answers will vary. C. u;
D. Answers will vary. E. I am going to be late!

Week 14, Day 1 (page 69)

A–B. Answers will vary. C. airplane;
D. Answers will vary. E. house/h, tie/t, yo-yo/y

Week 14, Day 2 (page 70)

A. shirt, cap, pants, shoe;
B–C. Answers will vary. D. n;
E. Answers will vary.

Week 14, Day 3 (page 71)

A. pan; B–C. Answers will vary.
D. circled in red: dentist, toothpaste; circled in blue: enamel, cavity;
E. Check students' circling.

Week 14, Day 4 (page 72)

A. Check students' handwriting;
B. Answers will vary. C. l;
D. Answers will vary. E. Did my cup spill everywhere?

Week 15, Day 1 (page 73)

A–B. Answers will vary. C. scissors;
D. Answers will vary. E. kite/k, sock/s, lamp/l

Week 15, Day 2 (page 74)

A. zebra, giraffe, tiger, elephant;
B–C. Answers will vary. D. o;
E. Answers will vary.

Week 15, Day 3 (page 75)

A. cake; B–C. Answers will vary.
D. circled in yellow: backyard, inside; circled in green: dishwasher, submarine;
E. Check students' circling.

Answer Key

Week 15, Day 4 (page 76)

A. Check students' handwriting;
B. Answers will vary. C. r;
D. Answers will vary. E. Ice melts and turns into water.

Week 16, Day 1 (page 77)

A–B. Answers will vary. C. window;
D. j. E. bib, bat

Week 16, Day 2 (page 78)

A. crayon, book, scissors, ruler;
B–C. Answers will vary. D. p;
E. Answers will vary.

Week 16, Day 3 (page 79)

A. ball; B–C. Answers will vary.
D. helicopter (4), butterfly (3),
yesterday (3), caterpillar (4);
E. Check students' circling.

Week 16, Day 4 (page 80)

A. Check students' handwriting;
B. Answers will vary. C. a;
D. Answers will vary. E. Yesterday was a very long day.

Week 17, Day 1 (page 81)

A–B. Answers will vary.
C. elephant; D. r; E. fan, pin

Week 17, Day 2 (page 82)

A. pig, horse, cow, chicken;
B–C. Answers will vary. D. q;
E. Answers will vary.

Week 17, Day 3 (page 83)

A. brush; B–C. Answers will vary.
D. umbrella (3), impossible (4),
discovery (4), basketball (3);
E. Check students' circling.

Week 17, Day 4 (page 84)

A. Check students' handwriting;
B. Answers will vary. C. r;
D. Answers will vary. E. How are we going to get there?

Week 18, Day 1 (page 85)

A–B. Answers will vary.
C. dinosaur; D. b; E. rat, bag

Week 18, Day 2 (page 86)

A. snowflake, scarf, mittens,
snowman; B–C. Answers will vary.
D. r; E. Answers will vary.

Week 18, Day 3 (page 87)

A. lip; B–C. Answers will vary.
D. computer (3), alligator (4),
potato (3) television (4); E. Check students' circling.

Week 18, Day 4 (page 88)

A. Check students' handwriting;
B. Answers will vary. C. b;
D. Answers will vary. E. Are we on the winning team?

Week 19, Day 1 (page 89)

A–B. Answers will vary.
C. basketball; D. s; E. net, hen

Answer Key

Week 19, Day 2 (page 90)

A. shark, whale, crab, starfish;
B–C. Answers will vary. D. s;
E. Answers will vary.

Week 19, Day 3 (page 91)

A. house; B–C. Answers will vary.
D. dinosaur (3), kindergarten (4),
dandelion (4), tricycle (3); E. Check
students' circling.

Week 19, Day 4 (page 92)

A. Check students' handwriting;
B. Answers will vary. C. n;
D. Answers will vary. E. I am
excited to go to the beach!

Week 20, Day 1 (page 93)

A–B. Answers will vary. C. camera;
D. n; E. wig, lip

Week 20, Day 2 (page 94)

A. fire, coffee, sunshine, lava;
B–C. Answers will vary. D. t;
E. Answers will vary.

Week 20, Day 3 (page 95)

A. mail; B–C. Answers will vary.
D. grasshopper (3), macaroni (4),
camera (3), cooperate (4);
E. Check students' circling.

Week 20, Day 4 (page 96)

A. Check students' handwriting;
B. Answers will vary. C. t;
D. Answers will vary. E. Can we go
eat lunch now?

Week 21, Day 1 (page 97)

A–B. Answers will vary.
C. motorcycle; D. d; E. mop, log

Week 21, Day 2 (page 98)

A. ladybug, cockroach, ant,
caterpillar; B–C. Answers will vary.
D. u; E. Answers will vary.

Week 21, Day 3 (page 99)

A. ape; B–C. Answers will vary.
D. happy/sad, up/down, boy/girl;
E. Check students' circling.

Week 21, Day 4 (page 100)

A. Check students' handwriting;
B. Answers will vary. C. w;
D. Answers will vary. E. I went to
the library today.

Week 22, Day 1 (page 101)

A. Answers will vary. B. a;
C. elevator; D. r; E. rug, bus

Week 22, Day 2 (page 102)

A. Answers will vary. B. loud;
C. Answers will vary. D. v;
E. Answers will vary.

Week 22, Day 3 (page 103)

A. in; B–C. Answers will vary.
D. hot/cold, awake/asleep, big/
small; E. Check students' circling.

Week 22, Day 4 (page 104)

A. Check students' handwriting;
B. Answers will vary. C. b;
D–E. Answers will vary.

Answer Key

Week 23, Day 1 (page 105)

A. Answers will vary. B. e;
C. helicopter; D. t; E. Check
students' work.

Week 23, Day 2 (page 106)

A. Answers will vary; B. smelly.
C. Answers will vary. D. w;
E. Answers will vary.

Week 23, Day 3 (page 107)

A. at; B–C. Answers will vary.
D. tall/short, correct/wrong, nice/
mean; E. Check students' circling.

Week 23, Day 4 (page 108)

A. Check students' handwriting;
B. Answers will vary. C. k;
D–E. Answers will vary.

Week 24, Day 1 (page 109)

A. Answers will vary. B. i;
C. alligator; D. l; E. Check students'
work.

Week 24, Day 2 (page 110)

A. Answers will vary; B. hard;
C. Answers will vary. D. X;
E. Answers will vary.

Week 24, Day 3 (page 111)

A. all; B–C. Answers will vary.
D. dark/light, day/night, dry/wet;
E. Check students' circling.

Week 24, Day 4 (page 112)

A. Check students' handwriting;
B. Answers will vary. C. d; D. at;
E. Answers will vary.

Week 25, Day 1 (page 113)

A. Answers will vary. B. o; C. kite;
D. f; E. Check students' work.

Week 25, Day 2 (page 114)

A. Answers will vary. B. quiet;
C. Answers will vary. D. y;
E. Answers will vary.

Week 25, Day 3 (page 115)

A. air; B–C. Answers will vary.
D. early/late, easy/hard, full/
empty; E. Check students' circling.

Week 25, Day 4 (page 116)

A. Check students' handwriting;
B. Answers will vary. C. g; D. my;
E. Answers will vary.

Week 26, Day 1 (page 117)

A. Answers will vary. B. u; C. cane;
D. d; E. Check students' work.

Week 26, Day 2 (page 118)

A. Answers will vary. B. hot;
C. Answers will vary. D. z;
E. Answers will vary.

Week 26, Day 3 (page 119)

A. mile; B–C. Answers will vary.
D. enter/exit, light/heavy, false/
true; E. Check students' circling.

Week 26, Day 4 (page 120)

A. Check students' handwriting;
B. Answers will vary. C. t; D. like;
E. Answers will vary.

Answer Key

Week 27, Day 1 (page 121)

A. Answers will vary. B. u; C. cape; D. short vowels: kit, can; long vowels: kite, cane; E. Check students' work.

Week 27, Day 2 (page 122)

A. Answers will vary; B. slow; C. Answers will vary. D. sh; E. Answers will vary.

Week 27, Day 3 (page 123)

A. lag; B–C. Answers will vary. D. fast/slow, near/far, left/right; E. Check students' circling.

Week 27, Day 4 (page 124)

A. I; B. Answers will vary. C. g; D. be; E. Answers will vary.

Week 28, Day 1 (page 125)

A. Answers will vary. B. o; C. pine; D. short vowels: cap, fin; long vowels: cape, fine; E. Check students' work.

Week 28, Day 2 (page 126)

A. Answers will vary. B. smooth; C. Answers will vary. D. th; E. Answers will vary.

Week 28, Day 3 (page 127)

A. tick; B–C. Answers will vary. D. first/last, float/sink, lost/found; E. Check students' circling.

Week 28, Day 4 (page 128)

A. me; B. Answers will vary. C. x; D. said; E. Answers will vary.

Week 29, Day 1 (page 129)

A. Answers will vary. B. a; C. fine, cube; D. short vowels: tub, hop; long vowels: hope, tube; E. Check students' work.

Week 29, Day 2 (page 130)

A. Answers will vary. B. large; C. Answers will vary. D. ch; E. Answers will vary.

Week 29, Day 3 (page 131)

A. tar; B–C. Answers will vary. D. soft/hard, give/take, go/stop; E. Check students' circling.

Week 29, Day 4 (page 132)

A. he; B. Answers will vary. C. l; D. do; E. Answers will vary.

Week 30, Day 1 (page 133)

A. Answers will vary. B. e; C. tube, made; D. short vowels: hug, mad; long vowels: made, huge; E. Check students' work.

Week 30, Day 2 (page 134)

A. Answers will vary. B. friendly; C. Answers will vary. D. wh; E. Answers will vary.

Week 30, Day 3 (page 135)

A. late; B–C. Answers will vary. D. high/low, short/long, in/out; E. Check students' circling.

Week 30, Day 4 (page 136)

A. that; B. Answers will vary. C. m; D. up; E. Answers will vary.

Answer Key

Week 31, Day 1 (page 137)

A. Answers will vary. B. i; C. bite, hope; D. short vowels: rat, man; long vowels: rate, mane; E. Check students' work.

Week 31, Day 2 (page 138)

A. Answers will vary. B. smell; C. Answers will vary. D. ph; E. Answers will vary.

Week 31, Day 3 (page 139)

A. nail; B–E. Answers will vary.

Week 31, Day 4 (page 140)

A. said, B. Answers will vary. C. n; D. it; E. Answers will vary.

Week 32, Day 1 (page 141)

A. Answers will vary. B. a; C. pipe, ride; D. short vowels: rag, tap; long vowels: tape, rage; E. Check students' work.

Week 32, Day 2 (page 142)

A. Answers will vary. B. run; C. Answers will vary. D. ck; E. Answers will vary.

Week 32, Day 3 (page 143)

A. me; B–E. Answers will vary.

Week 32, Day 4 (page 144)

A. The; B. Answers will vary. C. o; D. make; E. Answers will vary.

Week 33, Day 1 (page 145)

A. Answers will vary. B. i; C. cube; Sentences will vary. D. short vowels: fad, bit; long vowels: fade, bite; E. Check students' work.

Week 33, Day 2 (page 146)

A. Answers will vary. B. hop; C. Answers will vary. D. pl; E. Answers will vary.

Week 33, Day 3 (page 147)

A. to or too; B–E. Answers will vary.

Week 33, Day 4 (page 148)

A. my; B. Answers will vary. C. p; D. she; E. Answers will vary.

Week 34, Day 1 (page 149)

A. Answers will vary. B. u; C. huge; Sentences will vary. D. short vowels: pip, rip; long vowels: pipe, ripe; E. Check students' work.

Week 34, Day 2 (page 150)

A. Answers will vary. B. skate; C. Answers will vary. D. cr; E. Answers will vary.

Week 34, Day 3 (page 151)

A. bow; B–E. Answers will vary.

Week 34, Day 4 (page 152)

A. little; B. Answers will vary. C. r; D. who; E. Answers will vary.

Answer Key

Week 35, Day 1 (page 153)

A–B. Answers will vary. C. cute; Sentences will vary. D. short vowels: not, mop; long vowels: mope, note; E. Check students' work.

Week 35, Day 2 (page 154)

A. Answers will vary. B. color; C. Answers will vary. D. fl; E. Answers will vary.

Week 35, Day 3 (page 155)

A. pie; B–E. Answers will vary.

Week 35, Day 4 (page 156)

A. each; B. Answers will vary. C. s; D. there; E. Answers will vary.

Week 36, Day 1 (page 157)

A–B. Answers will vary. C. stars; D. apples; E. Check students' work.

Week 36, Day 2 (page 158)

A. Answers will vary. B. swim; C. Answers will vary. D. pr; E. Answers will vary.

Week 36, Day 3 (page 159)

A. pan; B–C. Answers will vary. D. s, so, som, some; E. Answers will vary.

Week 36, Day 4 (page 160)

A. more; B. Answers will vary. C. t; D. then; E. Answers will vary.

Week 37, Day 1 (page 161)

A–B. Answers will vary. C. bats; D. days; E. Check students' work.

Week 37, Day 2 (page 162)

A. Answers will vary. B. hug; C. Answers will vary. D. st; E. Answers will vary.

Week 37, Day 3 (page 163)

A. mouse; B–C. Answers will vary. D. l, li, lik, like; E. Answers will vary.

Week 37, Day 4 (page 164)

A. make; B. Answers will vary. C. r; D. your; E. Answers will vary.

Week 38, Day 1 (page 165)

A–B. Answers will vary. C. logs; D. lions; E. Check students' work.

Week 38, Day 2 (page 166)

A. Answers will vary. B. whisper; C. Answers will vary. D. tr; E. Answers will vary.

Week 38, Day 3 (page 167)

A. dish; B–C. Answers will vary. D. w, wi, wit, with; E. Answers will vary.

Week 38, Day 4 (page 168)

A. Would; B. Answers will vary. C. g; D. so; E. Answers will vary.

Week 39, Day 1 (page 169)

A–B. Answers will vary. C. rugs; D. clouds; E. Check students' work.

Week 39, Day 2 (page 170)

A. Answers will vary. B. spell; C. Answers will vary. D. fr; E. Answers will vary.

Answer Key

Week 39, Day 3 (page 171)

A. five; B–C. Answers will vary.
D. s, sa, sai, said; E. Answers
will vary.

Week 39, Day 4 (page 172)

A. if; B. Answers will vary. C. x;
D. from; E. Answers will vary.

Week 40, Day 1 (page 173)

A–B. Answers will vary. C. jars; D.
pencils; E. Check students' work.

Week 40, Day 2 (page 174)

A. Answers will vary. B. think;
C. Answers will vary. D. cr;
E. Answers will vary.

Week 40, Day 3 (page 175)

A. wig; B–C. Answers will vary.
D. y, yo, you, your; E. Answers
will vary.

Week 40, Day 4 (page 176)

A. from; B. Answers will vary. C. n;
D. am; E. Answers will vary.

Notes

_____

_____

_____

_____

_____

_____

_____

_____

_____

_____

_____